Low Life

Jeffrey Bernard

Duckworth

For Isabel Bernard
with love

Second paperback impression 1993
First Duckworth paperback edition 1992
First published in 1986 by
Gerald Duckworth & Co. Ltd.,
The Old Piano Factory,
48 Hoxton Square, London N1 6PB

ISBN 0 7156 2445 8

The main text of this book is
selected from Jeffrey Bernard's 'Low
Life' column in the *Spectator*.

A catalogue record for this book is available
from the British Library

Photoset in North Wales by
Derek Doyle & Associates, Mold, Clwyd
Printed and bound in Great Britain by
Redwood Books, Trowbridge, Wiltshire

LOW LIFE

Contents

Foreword
by John Osborne

'I have come to terms with the fact that my dinner is in the oven and always will be.'

Jeffrey Bernard is the Tony Hancock of journalism ('the Last Supper menu will be brown Windsor soup and minced beef with cabbage and boiled potatoes'), although his reports from the front of bullet-biting endured during his enforced periods of capture at the hands of a puritan and punitive medical profession are more harrowing than the fantasy loss of an armful of blood.

Unconstrained by lofty journalistic mannerisms, this collection of his columns in *The Spectator*, unlike most conceited cobbled 'books', has its own autobiographical momentum and unity. The sum, for once, is indeed greater than the weekly parts. There is live, squirming and bloody sinew beneath this continuing suicidal account of fragility. Failure – with women, drink, doctors, horses (the usual) – is transformed by his telling of it into a long, dark, heroic progress to the visible and disregarded underworld.

One turns first and naturally each Friday to 'Low Life'; the opening sentences can cheer the heart of every devout depressive: 'It's been a perfectly dreadful week ...', 'The past few days have been just about as bad as can be ...', 'For a moment I thought I was going mad ...', 'I wasn't feeling very well last week ...', 'On Monday I met a black bird with thrush ...'. Dateline: 'The Middlesex Hospital.'

His impeccable contempt is his energy: *Guardian* readers, Americans, the French, Fleet Street hackettes, spivs like André Previn and Michael Parkinson, *The Sun*, West Indian nurses, wheat germ and Joan of Arc, Real Ale, Bernard Levin, Jill Tweedie, Sir Peter Hall, electric typewriters, free-range women and the cruelties of marriage. The aim, fired from the shattered hip and prone in the gutter, like a dying bandit's, goes straight to the heart of the heartless.

He regains his feet from these pages, showing infinite gratitude to his possibly long-suffering friends, shaking himself all over them like a beloved Labrador. 'One of the things I loathed most about school, the army and regular employment was the feeling that I was missing something and that in the pubs, clubs, cafés, dives and racecourse bars there was some sort of magic in practice that I wasn't able to conjure with.'

But he did, and the unintimidated magic has never left him. His fantasies, at their most poetic, owe far more to Swift than to Smirnoff: 'I'd very much like to wake up one morning with a cow of the Friesian variety and walk her down to Soho to the Coach and Horses, stopping on the way to buy twenty Players, ply her with vodkas until closing time, whip her off to an Indian restaurant, take her up to the Colony Room till 5.30 and then to the Yorkminster, Swiss Tavern, Three Greyhounds, get beaten up by Chinese waiters at midnight, have a row with a taxi driver, set the bed on fire, put it out with tears and then wake up on the floor. Could you then milk the said cow? I doubt it.'

Jeffrey Bernard has always been that fine figure and bane of prigs, schoolmasters and pushy careerists, a Bad Influence. What such people always overlook is that the renegades they abhor so are the least likely to want to exert *influence*, of all things, whether by persuasion or example. Bad influences might be envied their irresponsible freedoms but not their forfeiture of approved opinion; the country is presently stuffed with every invented machinery imaginable, committees, boards and councils, all devoted to the folly of good influences.

'I most enjoyed the company of boys who were in trouble.' They were the irreverent ones who couldn't be fooled into accepting the solemn hokum of school life or the swotting, athletic toadies who would become the fearful workaholics, young executives and flash entrepreneurs of today.

Bernard is not merely a journalist, but a grim, brave and funny diarist of the times in which he is a snarling participant. And like all the most engaged historians, he has written his own epitaph to match the mood of those times: 'It stinks but it's the stink I know.'

He possesses courage and style in abundance and his eye for physical detail, both in delight and in distress, is as astonishing and stimulating as anything in Pepys or Boswell. The felicity of style has everything to do with courage. Alcohol has never seriously blighted an energetic or creative nature. It is workaholism that degrades and abuses commonsense. Workaholics Anonymous – I would drink to that any old day. Bernard sniffs out priggism, phoneys and officious banality like almost no one else: banal ambition which saps all proportion, seemliness, moral sense, and fires the mediocres, plodding and unscrupulous to everlasting vasty hells of covetousness and aggrandisement. 'I realised in those dives in Soho that there is no virtue in work for its own sake.' Such things should be known by any fool but seem only to reveal themselves to the weary but unvanquished wise.

To get to the business of drink: alcoholic is the pejorative which the thrusting achievers and the gravely concerned would apply to the likes of Bernard. He is a Heavy Drinker, in the company of Falstaff or Dr Johnson. Heavy Drinkers are not to be confused with alcoholics or modern drug-addicts. Heavy Drinkers may be often tiresome, boring and selfish, but love of good company and friendship is usually one of their saving gifts. If they make harsh demands, they give of themselves unreservedly. Sometimes the gift may be restricted to simply living their art rather than transmitting it into art or literature, but as often as not they do both. English literature would be pretty thinned down if it practitioners had paid heed to Government pamphlets on the dangers of drink. Coleridge may be a tricky advertisement for laudanum, but Smirnoff should boost its products as the blessed muse of Jeffrey Bernard.

How could one not love and admire a man who says: 'It was very soothing in much the same way as a cold lavatory pan is when pressed against the forehead when one is being sick. This happens frequently when opening buff envelopes.' The recognition is instantaneous. Or this about holidays: 'I can't wait for them and yet I am always pleased to get back to this rathole which I feel so safe in despite being surrounded by danger.' The messages pushed out from under the rathole door put us in debt to him, and all the duns, doctors and Inland Revenue Men should cross themselves and file abjectly away.

'I have met all sorts of sportsmen and I can tell you that boxers are the nicest.' This sounds to me as true as my own mild conviction that professional soldiers are more kindly and religious than clergymen.

Bernard is the man who would rather die than have the Abbey National anywhere near him, let alone *around* him, or be within drinking distance of that benighted majority who are 'safe because we are present and responsible'. Yet, as he points out, '*Both my feet are*

9

firmly on the ground. Best of all, I am not in the slightest bit frightened of opening buff envelopes.' He *is* frightened, as his grateful acknowledgement to the cooling properties of the lavatory rim testifies, but you know also that he will stand unsteady but alone like Custer until the last buff envelope impales his breast.

From drink and so to women. What he finds unbearable about women is that they are so resolutely in touch with reality. Romanticism could not be expressed more defiantly, ending not in the tears of others but his own. Romantics are poetry's gamblers and, true to form, he endearingly dwells on his winnings rather than his catastrophic losses. He cannot be accused of the vice of self-pity. He is too triumphant in celebrating his fleeting victories. The happy times are always in soft-focus and the result is always self-redeeming.

Because of this he feels impelled to say that perhaps he writes too much about *loss.* He doesn't, and those birth-marked with such a sense of loss can only grieve with him. Unlike my old grandmother who used to say, 'What you don't have you never miss', he lives daily with the heart's unease that does exactly that.

He knows too well the prurient pleasure that most of his readers derive from his bottled messages from the lower depths. It makes them feel safer. 'If you're living where the grass is greener it must be reassuring to glance occasionally at a rubbish dump.' No doubt the defiant flowers rising from it go unspotted. 'Not a lot actually happens to me,' he goes on. But it does, it does. '*I make things happen if I can.*' Which is exactly what every poet achieves and others rarely. 'I do, after all, like my friends, which is a lot more than I can say for a lot of the high-life brigade.'

His defiant losses are our jackpot.

John Osborne

Slightly rhyming verses for Jeff Bernard's 50th birthday

Elizabeth Smart died on 4 March. This poem first appeared in *In the Meantime* (Deneau, 1985).

My Dear Jeff,
I can't say enough
how much I admire
the way you have
conducted your entire
life, and the way you have
used your marvellous Muse.
And how right she was to
choose you. Because
she's a Rare Bird who would
have retired or died
if you hadn't known how
to amuse
her, and her you.
That's one non-bogus
marriage made
on Parnassus
and *true*.

She knew
exactly what and who
she was letting herself
in for: the real You.
Drink, betting shops and pubs
are the sort of thing that rubs
her up the right way;
she'll always stay
and make you more beautiful
and witty
every day.

This is a loose love
Ode, owed
to one of my friends
who is in my special
collection of people
who make amends
for endless excruciating
boring hours
so often lived
when foolishly pursuing
stimulation,
and none occurs.

Sterne, Benchley, Leacock,
Carroll, and Nash, and Lear
are not more dear
to me than bedrock
Bernard(3).
(Do I not pay 65p
ungrudgingly weekly,
for a fixative laugh,
uniquely Jeff?,
who has become
a consolatory
addictive to me?)

Wilde would have smiled
and been beguiled
and bright enough to know
that *you* had a better

11

Muse in tow
than he.
Could he see
the angelic emanations
from gutters where we
all fall, while
trying to pee,
and rise, or try to rise,
unwisely, in majesty?

And Swift is bitter
and cross
and doesn't make us
feel better
at bearing our lot,
and, in his rage
at the odds,
misses the old adage
that recurs to me
often, in every mess:
'against stupidity
even the gods
are helpless.'
He
lifted furious fists
but had no effect
on the jibbering idjits.

Your subject is not mean,
who's up, who's in,
or jockeying for position
(what a dreary sin).
Funny but kind,
your subject is justly seen
as the inexhaustible one
of nude mankind:
Yourself, in fact, drinking,
amidst the alien corn,
and explaining the amazing joke
of being born.

Your sources—

grief and love
and the Coach & Horses
and all the things we're
thinking of
but don't admit,
because they don't fit
our grand ideas of
our own importance.
You hit the
soul on the head
when it rises
out of its lying bed,
pompous with portents
above its station,
and greedy for rewards
above its ration.

But you're never snide,
and you never hurt,
and you wouldn't want to win
on a doctored beast,
and anyhow the least
of your pleasures
resides in paltry measures.

So guard, great joker God, please guard
this great Bernard,
and let 1982
be the most brilliant year he ever knew.
Let him be known
for the prince of men he is,
a master at taking out of
himself and us the piss.

If you will do this, God,
I'll be good all year,
and try to be better-dressed,
and soberer, and keep my prose-style clear,
(for this great man
is embedded in my heart)
I'll remain, Sir, then and only then,
Yours sincerely, Elizabeth Smart.

Introduction

I suppose I first got hooked on the low life as a child of about twelve and well before I really understood the meaning of the phrase. My initial taste and immediate liking for forbidden fruit was, I suppose, not simply a reaction against authority and rules but an instinctive feeling that there was something very, very exciting and possibly glamorous going on outside and beyond the walls of my playroom and schoolroom.

I'd had hints of it from an early age. My parents were what you might call middle-class Bohemian. My mother was an opera singer who came from a working-class family with vague gipsy origins. She had a touch of class when she sang and, although she toured America successfully with a company run by Sir Nigel Playfair, children and what she claimed was my father's jealousy cut her career short. My father was a stage designer, architect and designer of all sorts. He was quite an extraordinary man. He came from a family called Cornwallis-West who specialised in keeping skeletons in cupboards. There was a scandal connected with Jenny Churchill and they changed their name to Bernard. He sailed before the mast at the turn of the century and then got a job at the Manchester Opera House and taught himself to draw. At the end of the day he would take on local tearaways on the stage for nobbins – thrown in coins – at the instigation of the stage staff. Somehow, by his own grit and talent, he got to the dizzy heights of an office in Park Lane and a house in Cheyne Walk. Among other things he designed the Lyons Corner Houses and the entrance to the Strand Palace Hotel which now stands complete in the Victoria and Albert Museum. But my parents treated their children with some severity, and from the time my father died when I was seven years old my mother was hell-bent on giving me a good education in the hopes that I might become an officer and a gentleman.

But, as I say, during that time I saw too much evidence to go along enthusiastically with that venture. My mother gave occasional cocktail parties for musicians, actors and actresses and stage people of all sorts, and I didn't have to be more than twelve to see that they

13

were getting a little more fun out of life than the Latin master at my prep school or the local grocer in Holland Park. There was an atmosphere of a low life of sorts at home and it filtered down to me. I became aware of wickedness, and that's exactly what excited me about it. It needs to be said, to put it in perspective for readers too young to be of an age of awareness in the late 1940s, that almost everything one hankered for was considered wicked.

For us of course – not for parents or schoolmasters. Take sex. It was the age of suspender-belt and stocking. Only what they called 'broad-minded' people went to bed with anyone apart from their husband or wife. It was also extremely difficult indeed for a teenage boy to get a girl to bed at all, and if you were lucky enough it was quite something to boast about among your friends. You became an instant Jack the Lad. I used to think that only theatrical people and the working classes got drunk and that racing was strictly for the upper classes and villains. The prospects were sheer heaven and I couldn't wait to grow up.

Anyway, that was the backdrop for the first act of this farce called the low life. The second act opened with my discovery of masturbation. I knew nothing at all about sex and simply thought that masturbation was a unique discovery on my part that was a lonely hobby of a sort that produced a pleasant sensation. I introduced it to my incredibly innocent prep school the next term – feeling like Marco Polo returning to Europe with the new inventions of gunpowder and paper – and soon the entire school was rocked to its foundations both metaphorically and physically. Shortly after that I discovered the facts of sex itself: not so much life – sex. I found a handbook in some nearby woods issued to American GIs at the time. It was called *The Red Light*. Shortly after that I kissed a girl for the first time and what you might call the rot set in.

I passed my common entrance to a ghastly naval college called Pangbourne in the nick of time before being expelled for being what they called a bad influence. But, from then on, sex was uppermost in my mind and I spent two years sitting in the back row of a classroom with a picture of Veronica Lake and another of Ava Gardner pinned under my desk lid and speculating as to my first woman and the rest that, I hoped, might follow. Not a lot of work got done.

Now, it was at the same time that I discovered the Turf. I was barely aware of racing, but I did know that there was one boy who made a book and took sixpenny and shilling bets. Anyway, he was found out one day and the heavens opened up. He got no less than

My mother, Fedora, about 1925.

15

twelve cuts – cuts they were called in the navy and cut they literally bloody-well did because even wearing trousers my bum was bleeding. I was amazed. With schoolboy logic I thought anything you can get that lot for must be marvellous. Probably nearly as good as sex. So I started reading the racing pages.

At the same time as this I discovered the demon drink which, I hasten to add, wasn't to become any sort of a problem until years later. It wasn't a pleasure then, and nothing and no one is a problem until you get to need and love them.

At the beginning of one term, one of my friends brought back a bottle of rather disgusting cherry brandy. We sipped at it gently with two other boys at weekends in a hut in the woods we'd built. We used to sit in this hut, roll cigarettes and smoke while we discussed the various merits of Veronica Lake, Ava Gardner, Rita Hayworth, Gordon Richards and Charlie Smirke.

Looking back on those ghastly days I suppose one of the things that also attracted me to the low life eventually was the fact that I most enjoyed the company of boys who were always in trouble. I still do. But the future as an officer and gentleman came to an end when I was asked to leave. The Captain of the college sent my mother a letter asking her to take me away and in so doing paid me the greatest back-handed compliment I have ever received. 'While I consider him to be psychologically unsuitable for public school life,' he wrote, 'I consider he has a great future as a seam bowler.' What more could any low-lifer ask for setting out on the great journey of life?

So that was that. Authority and rules were slipping away fast, and suddenly all that delicious wickedness I had been dreaming about for years was within my reach: girls, pubs, clubs, racecourses and a room of one's own – bliss. With a pin-striped suit, all the rage in those days, I thought I could conquer them all. But then, for the first time, I became painfully aware of the business of money. I didn't yet realise that money meant something far more glorious – freedom. I was just acutely aware of the need for what we call 'moving-around' money.

But the base of operations I chose was Soho. I'd been there before in the school holiday when my brother, a student at St. Martin's School of Art, asked me up there for coffee one day. It was instant magic to me, a sort of Disneyland for low-lifers. There was a café they used that was full of artists, poets, amateur and professional philosophers, writers, actors, bums, layabouts, a few genuine

Bohemians, eccentrics, lunatics and pretty girls. There were also thieves, who then as now plundered Foyle's bookshop, ponces, bookies' runners and con men. It was heaven. Not the dreadful dump it is now. You can imagine what it was like suddenly to be plonked down in that after years of Dickensian schooling! But of course the endless cups of tea, the modest rent and the half pints of bitter even at only 8½d a half had to be paid for, and what on earth does an expensive but bad education equip you to do? Very little. So I began alternating between navvying and dish-washing, jacking the jobs in when I'd got hold of a few bob and then bumming around for a while until it was time to go to work again.

Now, let's get one thing straight about jobs like navvying and dish-washing. There are still people about who think that there's something vaguely romantic about hard graft like that. There isn't. Neither is there very much dignity in manual labour. If there was, the Duke of Westminster would be digging his own garden. The myth of the beauty of sweating your guts out comes from the romantic school of D.H. Lawrence-worshippers – and look where he ended up. Mexico. I worked in the coal mines in 1953 and one day on that wretched face I swore I would never look a page of his in the face again. People who like their jobs, people who – to use that awful sociological phrase, have 'job satisfaction' – may regard a stint on a building site as fun, but one of the first things I realised in those days in Soho was that there is no virtue in *work for its own sake*.

But anyway, between those lousy jobs there were some amazing times in Soho. It was extraordinary to go to Fitzrovia and drink with the faces of the fifties. There were the painters John Minton, the Roberts Colquhoun and McBryde, Francis Bacon – still with us. There was George Baker, Louis McNeice, the dreaded Dylan Thomas, Malcolm Arnold, Alan Rawsthorne. John Davenport, Tom Driberg, Maurice Richardson, Robert Newton – and one could go on. Actually, I'm not name dropping but simply pointing out the duality of that life. And it was the undercurrent of that life which was so incredibly appealing to me, the real low life, the mis-spent youth. There were snooker clubs and there was Jack Solomon's gym in Windmill Street. I got hooked on both snooker and boxing in those days. There were some marvellous fighters about then. I have met all sorts of sportsmen and I can tell you that boxers are the nicest. This may have something to do with the fact that when you can do it you don't have to be nasty. Boxing has gone to the dogs now, but then it had a touch of gladiatorial glamour about it. I used to train with champions in those days, world champions from America too, and they were all lovely men outside the ring. I progressed to working in a boxing booth in Tottenham – a very bent business except for taking on naive boys who wanted to show off in front of their girl friends – and for that I got the princely sum of ten shillings. Then I got a professional licence for a while – Jack the Lad again. The last fight I had was at Slough Town Hall. I got flattened and paid a fiver. Out of that I paid the return fare to Slough, ten bob to my manager and ten bob to my second. I shared the change with the loser of the main event on a bottle of Gordon's gin which we drank on the train home. This is the life, I thought. What a fool.

Of course, if I had listened to my mother I could have been a naval officer or learned how to become a bank manager or worked as a solicitor's clerk. And who the hell would I have met? As I've often said in the *Spectator*, I've met a better class of person in the gutter than I have in the drawing-room. That's not inverted snobbery, it's just that I prefer the company of people who know what it's like to be in the shit. Skating on thin ice keeps a man on his toes. My colleague Taki who writes the High Life column in the *Spectator* once said the only thing the rich can't buy is better company because, by virtue of being rich, they have to stick with each other.

But skating on thin ice wasn't a sport I took up seriously until I took up writing about racing professionally. As I said, I always liked it, but when I first had the expenses actually to go to the racecourse instead of the betting shop it gave me a hell of a buzz. In fact, until I got used to it, it almost made the hair on the back of my neck stand up. It's not easy to explain that. It has a sort of glamour. It has a sort of romance. A race can be extremely exciting. It's very colourful. It has a sort of electricity for me, but as usual words fail me. It's always difficult to communicate an enthusiasm or love. The people are something else. There are very few grey areas in racing. It's a black-and-white business. Racing people are either tremendously good people or they are out-and-out greedy sods. But there again, like my gutter – I use the word metaphorically, of course, and intend no insults – there are successful people in racing, not the privileged few, who started absolutely potless and who know just what it's like to be on the floor.

Now the whole point of mentioning this is to point out that the experience makes people *kinder*, and that's important. There's also the behind-the-scenes area in racing. You should go up on the Lambourn Downs early one spring morning when they're on the gallops riding work. If you stand on the top looking towards the village you can pick them out in the distance coming out of the mist. As they get closer the noise of the hooves comes through, and then as they slam those hooves into the turf it's like small thunder intermingled with the jangle of bits, bridles and stirrups, and the bellows of the horses' lungs, the air coming out of their nostrils like plumes on a cold bright morning. And they call *that* low life? If I was a poet I could convince you. Then, after that, you go down to the yard and have breakfast, and maybe Joe Mercer's there, or even Lester. Then it's cocktail hour and then off to the races. It's something of an alfresco drinking club, and that's the trouble.

When I was the *Sporting Life* columnist in 1971 you could say it was my downfall. Booze is the main artery that runs through the low life. Anyway, the column took on. I had my picture at the top of it twice a week and so strangers recognised me. They used to send me over everything from large scotches to bottles of champagne, and I'm afraid it went to my head in both senses of the word. In 1972, having been sacked from the *Life* because of my drunken behaviour, I ended up in what's politely called an alcohol and drug addiction unit attached to a lunatic asylum in Ealing.

It was pretty depressing. I had been a pretty heavy drinker since 1960, but with my involvement with racing five years later I really went over the top. At the time it all seemed rather jolly, but then I cracked after working for the *Sporting Life* and got carted off. The procedure in these places is to sedate you quite heavily on arrival, so that you avoid nasty withdrawal symptoms, and give you loads of vitamin B complex. You get woken up from time to time to get fed and they put you physically on your feet, so to speak. Even this trauma has its absurdities and lighter side.

When I did eventually come to on day three, I discovered that the man in the next bed to me was a BOAC pilot. I actually laughed after a week of tears. He'd landed a Trident at Heathrow so drunk that he'd passed out over the controls as soon as the plane had touched down. (This would make a fantastic television commercial.) Anyway, they grounded him in their infinite wisdom for a while, and later; would you believe, put him in charge of traffic control at Nairobi, where he somehow contrived to get two aircraft to land on the same runway at the same time, both coming in opposite directions. One of them had sufficient power to rise above it all at the last moment. I'm not sure whether you would call that high life or low life.

19

Anyway, Jumbo as he was aptly called, had had a rough time in the war and his drinking had been escalating ever since. But the funny thing was that nearly everyone in that place had an *excuse*. There was a singular lack of personality defects. Alcoholics are fantastic self-deceivers. The only prerequisite to stop drinking is to *want* to stop. The success of group therapy is wildly exaggerated, but then the medical profession don't really understand what goes on in an alcoholic's mind. Even Max Glatt, a world authority on the subject, once said to me, 'If you want to know about alcoholism ask an alcoholic.' But, over the years, it's a personal problem that I have come to accept without dramatising it – I hope. For me, it's just a bloody nuisance because it does interfere with the smooth running of one's day-to-day existence.

On the other hand, I wouldn't like day-to-day existence to be too smooth. That wouldn't go with low life at all. Perhaps the worst aspect of boozing is that it becomes one's first loyalty. And that's no exaggeration. That's why marriage is impossible. Drink is the other woman. Four times I've fooled myself into thinking I wanted to make a commitment of that sort, but I suppose what I'm really commited to are all the things I've been talking about. I'm never quite sure whether it has all been rather sad or rather ridiculous. It's certainly all absurd. A friend of mine who killed herself in a fire when she went to bed drunk and lit a cigarette used to say that you can't get through life without a highly developed sense of the absurd. I go along with that but, by God, she certainly had an absurd ending. I often think about her and two other friends who killed themselves falling down stairs and I'm sure that in a strange way people die when there simply isn't anything at all left for them to do.

The other thing I ponder sitting on my stool in the Coach & Horses is the alternative. The idle pub cliché-ridden chat often becomes unbearable when friends are absent and only the bores are holding the fort. 'How are you today? God, you look awful. What on earth was that fight about last night. Did you back Lester's in the last at Windsor? How did you get on with that woman I saw you talking to? Same again? Yes, I think I'll have just the one.' It makes me want to scream. And then I have this strange fantasy. You've seen those old posters advertising insurance. Well, I'm the man in one. I'm with my wife, a sweet, harmless, devoted little thing and we're striding forth purposefully into the future under a symbolic umbrella. We're safe because we're prudent and responsible. We've got the obligatory two children with us, a boy of fourteen and a girl of twelve

Mother as Carmen.

– decently spaced out – and they're beaming, he under his school cap and she in her gymslip. Behind us there's our little mock-Tudor house. I think we live either in Chislehurst or Haslemere. Apart from my loving family I love my lawn mower and my Ford Escort, which I lie under most Sunday mornings. I may have a glass of whisky and soda when I get back from the office, but I don't chew the cud with the lads down the local. I may have fifty pence on the Grand National, but both my feet are firmly on the ground. But, best of all, I am not in the slightest bit frightened of opening buff envelopes. In fact I'm not frightened of anything except possibly Mrs Thatcher losing the next election or there not being enough rain for the herbaceous border.

Now I'm not knocking this family, in fact I grudgingly envy them in some ways. The trouble is I can't find the family half way between that fantasy one and this single low one here that I've opted for. And speaking of families brings me to the delicate subject of women – although, heaven knows, they're about as delicate as an SS Panzer Division. Over the years it's been a strange sort of war between us, but now, well into the second half of the ridiculous game, they're leading me by the equivalent of six nil. But we've had some terrific truces. The sad thing is it nearly always ends in tears – mostly mine. In spite of that I must say that I've been very lucky in knowing some marvellous women and they've been very good to me. The clashes have been mostly over my selfishness and the fact that I can't bear the way most of them are so firmly in touch with reality. It is fairly typical of them that my favourite woman and wife said to me, when we split up, 'I thought you'd change and settle down.' I was drunk for most of the time I was wooing her, and surely you can see a train coming if you're standing on the line. Anyway, you don't change and settle down at 46.

Another trouble, I've always been at first attracted by the packaging, only to discover there was another person inside and not the one I'd dreamed of. Perhaps I'm caught in some sort of sartorial time-warp, or perhaps my tastes for appearances are somewhat dated. It's odd that winning stays in a gambler's memory for longer than losing does and I find it a little depressing that all the fringe miseries of being unable to make a relationship work stick vividly, whereas happy times in the mind's eye are now in soft focus. Perhaps it's because of that that I write so much, probably too much, about loss. This may be why some people enjoy reading about low life in the *Spectator*. It probably makes them feel safer. If you're living where the grass is greener it must be reassuring to glance occasionally at a rubbish dump.

Some women, though, seem to want to turn rubbish dumps into gardens. They also seem to like little-boys-lost. Well, at 52 I'm afraid that game's over, but I used to be quite good at it. But dear, oh dear, the things this obsession with women and sex led to in the past. It's utterly absurd, ridiculous and laughable to think that I've been through two spates of drunken suicide attempts over two different women. But then for years and years I was terrified of living alone and of the desolation of being left. It wasn't until quite recently that I discovered that being alone can often be a luxury.

The other thing I'm getting the hang of is building enough necessary arrogance of a sort to defend myself. It has to be reciprocal. If a person doesn't like you as much as you like them then they are quite simply, by definition, the wrong person. Playing Dante to a Beatrice isn't my idea of fun.

So what is my idea of fun? A lot of people can't understand why the idiom of low life interests me, since not a lot actually happens to me. I'm like a bee buzzing around finding flowers that have already had the honey taken. But it's not quite true. I make things happen if I can. For that matter what the hell actually *happens* in a bank, insurance office or to a shopkeeper? Not a lot.

I think the thing is to try to turn the day into an event somehow in whatever small way. Even being trapped by my addiction in a few pubs, clubs, restaurants and racecourses is a freedom of a sort, and I do, after all, like my friends, which is more than I can say for lot of the high-life brigade.

Anyway, from time to time I get tastes of the high life and I can't say I envy them for much except of course their money and that's only to provide more freedom. Steering a course between the high and the low is the best journey I know. A double life is my ideal, keeping them separate from each other. And that ideal is lived by a friend of mine, a famous contemporary painter. He works very hard from the crack of dawn and then mingles with low-lifers after lunch in the afternoon. Then, most evenings, he goes home, cleans up, puts on his Saville Row suit and goes out to very up-market or at least expensive clubs and restaurants, where he mingles with the aristocracy, rich and famous. I like the mixture. Meanwhile it's back to the Coach & Horses for me.

Dad designing at the Boston Opera House, 1912.

Happy days

I've just spent two days sitting on the floor surrounded by remorse-inducing memorabilia. Backache and boredom propelled me from my sick bed to clear up boxes and drawers full of old letters and papers, but it was the postcards and snaps, evidence of holidays and seemingly happier times past that ended up at grey Heathrow or with the slamming of a door – front and then car – that had me rooted to the carpet wondering for the millionth time what could or might have been. If you have tears, prepare to jerk them now. No, don't. It's been quite a laugh. I found an old divorce petition actually complaining that I was morose, sullen, non-communicative and shunning any social contact when I was *not* drinking; but what surprised me was the expression on the faces of those ladies in the holiday pics. You're standing there, a Mediterranean Jack-the-Lad under a palm tree with a long drink in one hand, peeling shoulders and self-conscious grin, and she, in spite of her sunny smile, has that look in her eyes, almost smouldering, denoting that all the while she can count the bills dropping on to the door mat at home. Fill in the balloon over her head and it would read, 'Why am I with this idiot?'

Pictures in which she or they are actually looking at you and not the camera are an even bigger giveaway. But what breaks my heart are the snaps that were taken at the time or just after you first met. Actually, they don't break my heart at all, they just make me cringe with embarrassment. There's that awful look of pride in new ownership that reminds me of a salesman with a new car or a child with a new dog. You're both sunny side up then and you think the process of hard-boiling is going to take a hundred years. But, sitting there on the carpet, pushing the snapshots to one side for a minute and dipping into the old letters, the tale unfolds itself. 'Miss you terribly.' 'So looking forward to next weekend.' 'We must try harder.' 'We can't go on like this.' 'I must have been mad to think it could work.' 'I think we should say goodbye.' Yes, your dinner might not be in the oven but, by Christ, your letters and snapshots are in your old drawers and scrapbooks.

Almost as sad is the sight of those old friends. There's Fred on the beach pulling a silly face, Jim pissed in a night club and Bob waving frantically from the balcony of his room. If you see Fred now – bump into him in a pub – he looks a little embarrassed. He assesses the situation, peering into your pocket with his X-ray eyes and asks, 'What are *you* doing now?' 'Oh, the same old thing,' you reply, resisting the temptation to remind him of the time he took you aside with tears in his eyes to tell you that Maggie was leaving him and that life was no longer worth living. 'Still scribbling?' he asks, adding, 'No, no. I insist. This one's on me.' The largesse is so offhand and who'd think the four of you once squabbled over a restaurant bill in Paris?

With luck and in two or three weeks' time I'm off to get a breath of sun-drenched hot air into the offending lung. Alone. But I shall still take a camera. Three years ago I got a Russian soldier in Red Square to take a picture of me standing outside the Kremlin. It's deeply moving. I look like another alcoholic defector. But however awful one looks the memory banks and scrapbooks need to be kept stoked up. The holiday show must go on. This time I'll get a snap with the local barman. We'll have our arms around each other's shoulders and if you look carefully and closely into his eyes you'll see that he's thinking, 'God, how I loathe these boring, drunken, peseta-less tourists.' The only trouble is that I may not be drunk. At the moment I can hardly keep one down, so you'll forgive me I hope if I remain yours, morose, sullen, non-communicative and shunning any social contact. That wife was quite right about not drinking. It's disaster. If you're born two or three drinks under par you just end up with your old snaps snapping at people.

Lone Christmas

Turkeys, I suppose, spend the major part of their lives being lulled into a false sense of security and well-being. Their final demand, so to speak, comes but once and lack of rehearsals must make the final crunch an unexpected and painless event. No, I can't feel sorry for them en masse but I couldn't help shedding a tear for the one I nibbled at in the Park Lane Hilton on Christmas Day. The idea of being stuffed daily only to end up being eaten by me and an assorted bunch of fairly revolting Arabs and Iranians makes me feel that a turkey's life lacks meaning. And, talking of getting stuffed, it occurred to me as I eyed the menu that had the Last Supper been held in the Hilton the bill would have come to £500, VAT and tip included.

But it was a pretty good lunch as lunches go, even though conversation was limited to exchanges with a trainee wine waiter who'd just learnt the phrase 'full-bodied' and who kept repeating it like a parrot. I had a nice little table by the window on the first floor restaurant that overlooked Hyde Park. The grass there was like icing on an enormous cake. To my right the sun was setting over Byron's statue and to my left a hideous Arabian couple were looking down their amazing noses at me and getting high on Evian Water. You can hardly blame Arabs for making their women cover their faces but you can certainly blame the men themselves for dressing in those horribly common, expensive Yves St Laurent suits that still have flared trousers. They marinate themselves in Fabergé after-shave and talk constantly of money. The idea of being whipped by these people for having the odd drink gave me the most dreadful daymares, and I shall be turning down any offers from the *Kuwait Times* to syndicate Low Life.

The population of the Hilton made me feel I was residing in the Gaza strip and they could have saved themselves fortunes if they'd put down sand instead of carpets. Behind me, a Jewish couple spent the lunch talking, not to each other, but to the waiters. 'A sausage with your stuffing, sir?' – 'Ooh, no. My husband won't eat sausages – will you, Cyril? No, he's always hated sausages, haven't you? I've tried him on sausages time and time again, but he just won't eat one – will you darling?' In the background an incredibly naive and old-world pianist was getting little response from the ivories he was tickling heavy-handedly. He played a strange non-stop medley that comprised such leaden oldies as 'Old Man River', 'Hearts of Oak', 'Polly Wolly Doodle' and 'Rock-a-Bye Baby'.

I kicked off with an avocado, which was followed by some excellent chicken consommé. With the last sip of that, between 'Jingle Bells' and 'You Made Me Love You', a big table in front of me was taken over by a very flash Italian family. The woman immediately put me off the forthcoming turkey. She was one of those blonde icebergs I'm irresistibly drawn to and who make me feel like the *Titanic*. The packaging is obvious. Butter wouldn't melt in their mouths but gold ingots might. They wear on their backs what they've earned on them and at 40 the skin begins to wrinkle around the eyes with the effort of trying to acquire even more wealth and ease. Even the children have blow-waved hair and are allowed to snap at waiters. Well, I staggered through the main course eyeing the lady's excellent legs, but my food was out of focus since I'd lost my reading and eating glasses. Over three hours at my table I consumed a modest bottle of Moulin à Vent and one large vodka. That lot came to £19.05, which I thought was pretty strong, and I also thought I was being rather nice to the *Spectator* accounts department by eschewing the wine that cost £200 a bottle. The lunch was £25, by the way. I came back to earth over the pudding. As I say, I'd lost my glasses and the waiter didn't bother to tell me that the first mouthful was still on fire. But the Hilton food is good, and the simple meal I had that night – a hamburger and chips followed by a fresh fruit salad and two drinks – was even better, although I thought £10.85 a trifle steep with 15 per cent on that.

No, where these people get you is over trifling items like 30p for a very brief telephone call. Also, another entry, 'Room service dinner – £5.40', was simply a drink and a piece of cake, if my memory serves me, which it doesn't often. And although the room was very comfortable, I thought £77 a little much. But then I'm not, like the foreign guests, in a position to regard loot as mere pieces of paper. As a lone Christmas I preferred it to being alone at home. After all it was amusing to watch other people putting such an enormous effort into a ritual that's Double Dutch to them. They looked quite incredulous when Father Christmas walked into the restaurant ringing a bell and actually giving the children presents. When I signed the bill on Boxing Day morning, all I could think of was the fact that had Pontius Pilate had any sense at all and simply put Jesus Christ on probation for a couple of years or given him a suspended sentence, then none of this would have happened.

Heroes

Let us now praise the heroes of 1985. First there was Stanley. Now Stanley's a good man. True he drinks a little and true his marriage was on the rocks because of it, but he made an effort, did Stanley,

Middle row, far left, the would-be Harold Larwood in 1946.

and one day last summer he told his long-suffering wife that he'd bought tickets to South Africa where they'd go for a holiday. A second honeymoon if you like, a new start, a new leaf and the slate would be clean. Well, why not? Give it a go, she thought.

Came the day they were to depart from Heathrow and Stanley had just one more little thing to do and that was to take his office staff to luncheon. His good wife was to pick him up at the restaurant at 3 p.m. and off they'd go. Of course, by then dear Stanley was legless having had, by the wine waiter's reckoning, 12 Remy Martins on top of the obligatory plonk. Never mind, she thought, give him one more chance. Once on the flight and once in Africa he'd be all right. Off they drove to Heathrow, Stanley hiccupping gently all the way and nodding off from time to time, and eventually they got to the check-in point where Stanley was promptly sick all over the girl who

29

was doing the checking in. Still, his wife went along with him. Not so the airline people. At the last moment they refused Stanley a boarding pass. Now, I for one would give Stanley ten out of ten for effort. Whether or not a safari by water wagon would have saved Stanley's marriage is neither here nor there. The fact remains there was true nobility in Stanley having bought two tickets to South Africa, let alone leaving the safety of the restaurant for the hazards of flight, and I'd willingly go into the jungle with him and probably will.

And let us not forget the heroines of yesteryear. What about Eva? This extremely practical and sensible woman seduced one of England's leading bookmakers after the last race of the Royal Ascot meeting. A nasty man who refused me credit once when I was under tremendous pressure, he fancies himself as being a staying satyr brimful of stamina. In fact, as Eva later told me, he's a sexual bore. Anyway, into bed they got and after an hour and a half of making love to her he was still making love to her and, as she shrewdly observed, you can have too much of a good thing. So she turned on the bedside light and began to read *Middlemarch*. Came the dawn and the collapse of the revolting penciller she'd ploughed through five chapters. A tremendous compliment to George Eliot, don't you think?

Another who did well last year was Michael Nolles who fell down the concrete stairs to his basement flat. Yes, he fell head over heels, breaking a leg badly and landing outside the door of his flat. His wife, hearing his moans, opened the door – which opened outwards – and smashed his head in. Then, assuming he was drunk, she closed the door and left him there. By morning, hypothermia had set in. He now limps with a touch of humility and is hoping to buy a bungalow.

And, lest we forget, Jeremy. Since I reported trying to get him back into the Queen's Elm he has been barred from the Cadogan Arms, Finches, the wine bar next to it and been shown the yellow card by the Coach & Horses and the Man in the Moon. As a psychiatrist once told me, geographical escapes are futile, but I can see no alternative for Jeremy and I must recommend Northampton which has, I'm told, more pubs to the acre than any town in England.

And I'm still getting reports of the late lamented and lovable Michael Dempsey. Last week a colleague told me that on the occasion of Michael's last visit to Ireland he stayed in a town which boasted some thirty pubs. Within two days, Michael was considered to be a poet, gentleman and scholar in five of them and barred from four others.

Dempsey's last bow was more spectacular in my opinion than Sherlock Holmes' at the Reichenbach Falls. One of his last public appearances was made at the Lamb & Flag in Lamb's Conduit Street. Faced by a bevy of the Right to Choose Party, he said, 'I'm glad to see that you are all wearing your Right to Choose badges. This means that you are all opting to have abortions. In that case, you will not be producing children who are as hideous and revolting as yourselves.'

Cards

It's been a perfectly dreadful week relieved only by the reappearance of Tom Baker, who's finished his stint in *Treasure Island* and survived the dreadful parrot, and I've decided definitely to give up playing poker on Thursday nights. Everyone thinks they can play poker. It's a sort of Mitty thing. The green baize, the cigar-smoke haze, the occasional clink of ice in the glass breaking the tense silence or the flick and snap of a card and the superb feeling of filling a straight before pulling that pile of money towards you. Well, my Thursday night games haven't been quite like that. For one thing we have a Spanish waiter who's quite mad and who can turn a pair of fives into a drama on a par with *Aïda*, and for another there's a tendency for people to turn up at 8 p.m. far too smashed to make any sense of the game. Admittedly it's a friendly game in so far as we all start with a lousy £10-worth of 10p pieces but where's the romance in winning – no, losing – £10? I felt so ghastly the morning after the last game I thought I would go in search of one card who could cheer me up, Peter Langan. Sadly he wasn't in his little Brasserie – he's driving the population of Los Angeles mad at the moment – but I had a drink at the bar and reflected on what an extraordinary man he is. He has style, you know. Some time ago there was a fire in the kitchen. They dialled 999 and sent for the Fire Brigade. While they awaited the firemen Langan tried to keep the fire under control with champagne. I'm not claiming that it was Louis Roederer Cristal Brut, neither is he, but it does indicate a certain amount of imagination and a healthy contempt for wine with bubbles in it.

Which reminds me of the story I heard of another card who shall have to remain nameless, but a restaurateur as well. This man arrived home at six in the morning after a night on the tiles, totally legless and bursting for a pee. He fell out of his taxi and just as he was about to urinate in desperation into the gutter he spotted a dear old couple approaching who were taking their dog for an early morning trot. A vestige of decorum prompted him to do the decent thing and he turned away. As the seconds went by he became more desperate and stumbling up the steps to his front door he aimed his keys at the lock which he missed and missed again. He was now at his wits' end – no great distance to travel – and he inserted his member through the letterbox. Now, it so happens that at that precise moment his landlord, an angry man who had been trying to evict our hero for some time, was walking down the staircase with his dog, with the perfectly reasonable intention of taking some exercise. You may imagine his and Fido's horror when confronted not with the terror of a buff envelope but with our man's member. The hound backed snarling and steaming, the landlord – one can only imagine – clasped his fluttering heart and our man politely turned his head to say 'Good morning' to the couple he had originally tried to avoid offending. There has to be a moral somewhere but I'm damned if I can see it.

Yes, the Soho cards are a lot better than the ones I've been dealt at the tables recently, which reminds me ... Brian's just been sprung after 16 months inside. I hear he didn't have too bad a time of it since they put him in charge of the kitchen – surely, the library apart, the cushiest job in the nick and the best place in which to fiddle therein. It'll be cheering to see him again. Meanwhile, here in the Coach & Horses depression sets in again. As I write to you at my desk in the saloon a Maltese gentleman at my side is actually studying the Crayford and Bristol greyhound racing cards in the *Sun*. I ask you. Dogs – Crayford – Bristol – the *Sun*. Is this the end of civilisation as we know it? You could slam the letterbox on the member of such a man.

Unbalanced

The past few days have been just about as bad as bad can be. I'm still getting some nasty twinges because of the man who cut off his penis. Yes, if you didn't happen to see it in the papers this man cut off his penis and threw it on the fire so that he could devote the rest of his life to God without any distractions. It seems that he and his wife had been discussing the horrific business for the past twelve years and last week he took the plunge. With her blessing, wouldn't you know. Well, I've been pondering aspects of this bizarre do-it-yourself surgery and some interesting points arise apart from the very obvious fact that the wife must be a *Guardian* reader (she's probably already received her 'Jill'll Fix It' badge).

But why did the wretched man choose his perfectly harmless penis? Surely he must have realised that sex is in the head and that his penis was merely his solo instrument in a far bigger concerto than you or I will ever comprehend. I mean, if I wanted to devote the rest of my life to any one thing at all without being distracted I'd cut off my head. Then, of course, I can't help wondering what their sex life must have been like during the past twelve years of disarmament talks. Pretty tentative I should think and, with the thought of the dreadful redundancy to come in the back of his mind, maybe non-existent. And another thing, why dispose of the black-balled would-be member on a fire? What on earth does he think waste-paper baskets are for? I suppose he was committing it to hell. And then, in spite of what must have been considerable post-operative pain, he discharged himself from hospital after only three days – that is, if a man sans penis can discharge himself at all.

The fact that God didn't intervene in the matter proves my theory that He is a woman after all. But what a typically selfish woman that wife. You wouldn't want to go into the jungle with her. I mean, she could have cut off something herself, even it had only been her hair, just to show willing. What a Grimm business. If the silly man had never got married in the first place he would only have had to cut off his right arm, assuming he's right-handed that is.

What a mug. Wouldn't you be suspicious? I can just imagine a wife saying to me, 'Now, come along. Be a darling and cut it off.' I'd think, 'Now hang on a minute. Is she trying to tell me something? Is this some sort of clue?' I'm not daft, you know. And another thing. If you were in his boots having done the deed how would you feel if you saw your renegade wife chatting up the milkman? There's a possible television comedy series in this.

Another criticism I have to make about this now top-heavy evangelist is that to take twelve years to make up one's mind about anything shows a certain lack of resolution. If I was lying in my bath feeling slightly disgruntled and pondering a penisectomy I'd do it there and then. Or would I? Perhaps not. Whereas his pruning was quite ruthless, I'd probably chicken out and take it an inch at a time.

So, where will he go from here? What will guide him? Speaking for myself – a bad habit I must get out of – I'm where I am today having followed for 30-odd years the direction in which my penis has pointed. The resultant emotional aggravation has been colossal, but I wouldn't have done without it. The aggravation I mean. How slow, calm and tedious would the rat race be if none of us jockeys had whips.

Yes, as I say, it's been a horrid week and I can't help wondering whether our man has had second thoughts. Dear God, it's a sad life. What people do to each other is bad enough. Now I'm beginning to think that madness is self-inflicted. Never trust a man who's not grateful for small mercies.

Poles apart

For a moment I thought I was going mad. There I was, sitting quietly in the Coach & Horses minding my own business and having my 11 a.m. gargle, when this man walked up to me and said, 'D'you remember Peter the Pole who worked in the dirty bookshop in St Anne's Court? You know, the bloke whose father is an ear-nose-and-throat surgeon in Warsaw? Well anyway, he's just moved to Hounslow.' There's no answer to that. It has to be the most extraordinary address I've ever had aimed at me. Not only do I not know Peter the Pole, have never even heard of him, nor care greatly how his father scrapes a living, I also have very little time for

Robert McBryde and Robert Colquhoun in their Bedford Gardens studio in 1948.

a man who moves to Hounslow and wouldn't trust him an inch. But what an amazing thing to walk up to someone out of the blue and ask them that.

So I said no, I didn't know the said Peter the Pole, and I turned my back on the man – feeling distinctly apprehensive – and continued to ponder the meaning of life and man's incredible ascent from the discovery of fire and the invention of the wheel to Hounslow.

Well might I have been apprehensive. Just as I was beginning to feel a little calmer the charming Mrs Balon, Norman's unfortunate mother, snuck up behind me and whispered, 'I bet you didn't know my grandfather had an umbrella shop in Gower Street.' Oddly enough the possibility of Mrs Balon's grandfather ever having had an umbrella shop in Gower Street has never crossed my seething brain, although, God knows, I'm a broad-minded man. Well, after a short but emotional discussion on the subject of the 1890 umbrella boom in Gower Street, Mrs Balon and I went out separate ways: she to the snack bar and me back to what was rapidly becoming a strictly medicinal drink. Just as I was draining that, a man approached me and said, with a thick Glaswegian accent, 'Hey Jimmy, I bet you've never seen a black man's funeral.'

Then it clicked. I was in the middle of some dreadful plot. These mad utterances were codes or ciphers like the Thirty-nine Steps or the Five Orange Pips or the Dancing Men. Obviously I was to meet a man with a Polish accent in Hounslow who would give me a message to deliver to a dead black man in an umbrella shop in Gower Street. Nothing so extraordinary about that after all, is there? But it called for another drink, and just as I ordered it the Glaswegian sprang at me again. 'No, you haven't,' he said. 'When they die they make them into tyres.'

Long-distance

If one needed proof of the stupidity of Americans beyond the democratic election of both Mr Carter and Mr Reagan then surely Heaven's Union, the celestial telegram service run by a Gabriel Gabor, is just that. In case you didn't read about it the idea is that you send a telegram of up to fifty words to relatives and friends who've heard the guvnor in the sky call 'last orders' and who've subsequently departed for the Great Beyond. The messengers who carry these mad messages are terminally ill patients who memorise them before they snuff it and Mr Gabor cops £23 for each one. I find it fairly sick.

'How d'you do. I hear you're dying. Jolly good. Well done. Look, I wonder if you'd do me a favour and ask my wife where she left my gold cufflinks. I'll pay for a reply which you can give to a baby that's going to be born after you get there. And oh, by the way, while you're there ask her was she being knocked off by Bill Smith. Thanks. Have a good trip.'

But that's not all Mr Gabor has up his sleeve. He's got talking tombstones. Before your missus pegs out she records a message on to tape and then, when you visit her grave on a Sunday afternoon to put a vase of dandelions on it, you press a button and, lo, you hear the same old story again. 'Hello, is that you Jeff? I'm amazed you managed to tear yourself away from the pub to come and visit me. Your dinner's in the oven. Honestly, I thought you'd change and settle down. Don't you ever think of the future. Christ, this headache is killing me. I suppose you lost it all at the betting shop. Stop staring at that woman at the next grave. You're drunk again. You make me sick. Don't bother to come next Sunday. I'll be all right. Don't worry about me. I don't suppose you ever have, anyway. Always thinking about yourself. Me, me, me. I told you you make me sick, didn't I? Yes, of course I did. Well, good bloody bye.'

Mind you, the chances of outliving a wife are pretty remote, so I don't think the question will arise and I'm wondering if Mr Gabor has any messengers bound for hell. I'm delaying the trip there for as long as possible myself but should any readers care to send me £23 I'm willing to drive over Beachy Head after one final fling. Yes, I'm definitely not going to heaven. I'm sure it's very white and cold, sparsely furnished with maybe a bit of shining chrome here and there and altogether rather like a modern hospital. I suppose they sit about in little groups talking about the old days and gesticulating limply with their wings and enquiring of all newcomers, 'Any messages?'

Yes, I don't think hell will be a lot different from where I'm at now. In fact I'm fairly well convinced that I died in 1932 and this is it. I mean, just look at Norman in the Coach. All he needs is a trident in one hand – I must get him to take his shoes off to see if he's got cloven hooves – and there's your devil. God knows, most of the customers are griffins and gargoyles or advocates and I'm certainly getting my fair share of messages. I particularly like the ones I get on the phone when Mum Balon answers it and asks me across the room, having forgotten to cover the receiver, 'Are you here?' 'Who is it?' 'I don't *think* he's here but he says who is it.'

But this American business; they've got to be mad. A psychologist who counsels the terminally ill in Los Angeles says of Mr Gabor's message service: 'It could provide the dying with a sense of purpose.' That's a great bloody comfort. I'm pretty sure I'm dying and my purpose is to hang on to life. Like grim death.

Questionable

Two weeks ago *The Times* carried another of those silly, melodramatic features on the subject of alcoholism. It was headed by the usual old questions which, if you could answer yes to any of them, showed that there was 'serious cause for alarm'. Well, the more I looked at these questions the less alarmed I felt. In fact I've now come to the conclusion that I don't drink enough. Just look at this nonsense.

Q. *Do you find that you drink embarrassingly quickly and have finished your drink long before those around you?*

J.B. The speed at which I drink embarrasses others. That's to say I am frequently outfumbled. Peter Owen, for example, last bought a round in 1971. Such men need to be reminded that one swallow does not make a summer.

Q. *Do you have time off from work because of drinking; or has your work performance suffered because of alcohol?*

J.B. The situation is very much the reverse. Work frequently interferes with my drinking. Last week I spent an hour drinking Perrier before going to see a publisher, while all around me were falling down. And another thing. Drinking *is* my work. I was once paid £500 for an article on that very subject.

Q. *Do your family and friends express concern over the amount you drink?*

J.B. Well, as my big brother says, 'Concern is a very elastic word.' I think they express a mild surprise at where on earth the money comes from and they simply look into their glasses a little harder. My friend, the philanthropist and thespian Tom Baker, is concerned that I don't drink enough. He says that if I could get a bit more vodka in I might spew up a novel.

Q. *Have there been family quarrels because of your drinking? Are you becoming difficult, irritable and testy after drinking?*

J.B. I believe there was a tremendous row in 1934 as to whether I should be fed Nestles or Cow & Gate milk. Am I *becoming* difficult, testy and irritable? You must be joking. I'm impossible. After closing time last Tuesday I hit a Greek greengrocer in Goodge Street who asked me not to feel his cucumbers. I also have three ex-wives who can testify to my testiness. Especially *before* drinking.

Q. *Do you find that your memory is getting worse? Have you ever had loss of memory after a heavy drinking session?*

J.B. Quite honestly I can't remember ever having had a heavy drinking session. Can you repeat the question please?

Q. *Do you order yourself a double when the rest of the party are drinking singles, or do you order yourself a quick extra drink while collecting an order from the bar?*

J.B. None of my 'party' drinks singles. They do have some style,

With my oldest friend, Pete Arthy, in the Mandrake Club in 1949.
Delinquent days.

you know. As to ordering a quick drink I can tell you that there is no
such thing in either the French Pub or the Coach & Horses. Both the
barman in the French and Michael in the Coach take more time to
serve a drink than it took the Royal Navy to get to the Falkland
Islands.

Q. *Do you have an uneasy feeling that you are drinking too much; that you
no longer have control over your drinking; that you can no longer take it or leave
it?*

J.B. No, but I do have an uneasy feeling that I won't be able to
take it for much longer. I live in dread of hepatitis and the obligatory
six months' abstention that follows it.

Q. *Has your sexual drive and ability suffered because of your drinking?*

J.B. Mind your own fucking business. Actually, I find alcohol to
be an aphrodisiac. Especially for the duration of a hangover.
Unfortunately, since I discovered Smirnoff – and this is an
unsolicited testimonial – I no longer get hangovers.

Q. Do you ....?
J.B. I'm sorry, I can't answer any more questions. It's nearly opening time.

Wanderlust

I'm thinking, quite seriously, of retiring. The list of things I haven't done is far too long and I'm well into the second half of this ridiculous game. While I was sitting on a train last weekend and gazing out of the window at Oxfordshire and Berkshire it occurred to me, for example, that I've never fished or lazed my way up the Thames in a luxury cabin cruiser crewed by voluptuous young women. Who needs a desk and a typewriter? Neither have I whiled away the day on a golf course and in the club house. Yes, the sight of the River Thames, even in dreaded Pangbourne of ghastly memories, had me dreaming of picnic hampers in bee-loud glades by quiet waters, chilled white wine and pâté under summer skies, no deadlines just fishing lines and distant girlish laughter, but not too distant of course.

Weather permitting, my intention this summer is to take a boat from Reading to Oxford, stopping at every pub and decent restaurant on the way. Whether I shall make the trip before or after my Greek holiday I'm not sure. Yes, a delightful friend of a friend I met at the weekend has put his villa and yacht at my disposal and I think I might throw this typewriter out of the window in a few minutes' time. Neither have I sipped raki in Istanbul or fed peacocks in Kashmir, and Mexico beckons. True, I've eaten bread and dripping in Camden Town and downed a half of bitter in Notting Hill, but I shall be 50 in two weeks' time and I haven't sailed up the Nile or seen Hong Kong – in fact, the highlights so far have been pretty dim. Had I video replays to command, the choices would be fairly sparse. They certainly wouldn't concern *any* work I've ever done, except for three months with Joan Littlewood, but I would like to see playbacks of my wedding days just to remind me of the fund of optimism I once had. Why the sight of the Thames should trigger off these middle-aged meanderings I'm not quite sure, but it did and I'd very much like to tie an apple in my handkerchief and take a walk around the world. I suppose the sight of the water got me thinking of boats, then ships, and I can stare at cargo ships all day dreaming and wondering where they've been and where they're going. As for staring into the mirror, a pastime less compulsive than it used to be, I can see exactly where I've been and where I'm going and the impending birthday which has recently become an obsession is concentrating my mind horribly.

Readers wishing to commit suicide are invited apply for berths on the good ship *Miss Right* sailing up the Thames sometime in July. Whether there'll be room for you all I'm not sure, but if you're feeling anything like me we might have to get a bigger boat, as the man said in *Jaws*. In that event we could conclude this entertainment in the blue of the Mediterranean. Dave in the French pub has suggested time and time again that we hire a bus and drive over Beachy Head, but I think it lacks style.

It could have been a glimpse of the boathouse at Pangbourne where I used to smoke illicit cigarettes that got me going for, after all, time's stood still since then. One's still smoking illicit cigarettes, so to speak, but it's just that one no longer cares about being caught. Come to think of it quite a few of us were caught a long time ago. So, is it too late to take early retirement and trail our hands in the waters of the Thames? Not if we hurry and act now. I call on all of you who aren't enjoying your work to give up. Take the cotton wool out of your ears and *listen* to the sirens. Join me on the rocks. Meanwhile, I shall contemplate further on the business of being 50, have a good cry and a drink. Not necessarily in that order.

Candidates

If you answered that extraordinary Dateline computer dating ad with absolute honesty I wonder what on earth you'd get. Well, I don't. I mean I wonder what *I'd* get. They ask, in the bit you fill in and send off to them, 'Do you consider yourself Shy, Extrovert, Adventurous, Family Type, Clothes-conscious, Generous, Outdoor Type, Creative, Practical, Intellectual.' Then the loons go on to say, 'Indicate which activities and interests you enjoy' etc, and they list a load of guff whereby you could con anyone from a distance and land yourself a meet with something really awful.

Now, one is fairly civilised and likes classical music and poetry and knows that there's nothing like half an hour's chat with the barman on the subject of the polyphonic motets of Lassus, but who on earth wants to meet a woman whose idea of a swinging weekend is two hours in the British Museum Reading Room followed by a nut cutlet picnic in the park reading Keats out loud before setting off for an archaeological dig with knapsacks stuffed with tapes of the Matthew Passion, *Under Milk Wood* and the late quartets? I have a vision of pitching a tent by the dig, diverting her attention by pointing out a lesser crested grebe, quickly going through her handbag and discovering she's not on the pill. Thank you and goodnight. You could tell a woman like that that it was opening time and she'd think you were talking about the British Film Institute.

On the other hand, if you ticked off, in the list of activities and interests, Pubs and Clubs, Jazz, Sport, Good Food and Travelling you'd be landed with an equally ghastly disaster area. She'd almost certainly have laddered stockings, eyes that had worked overtime at crying, a handbag containing a rubbish dump, thrush, a smoker's cough, an Equity card, and a bedsitter with a single bed in Clapham. (Sorry about the Clapham bit, Sheila.)

But the list of what you may consider yourself to be is a trifle daft, not to say short. Shy? Extrovert? Well, both of course. Generous? Yes, and mean and selfish too. Outdoor type? Well I've never found a secret tunnel to the Coach & Horses, but I have occasionally managed to unwind in the gutter after a hard day's work. What about Family Type? I've tried to start more families than you've had hot dinners, madam. Clothes-conscious? I am aware of the fact that they're mostly on the floor and under the bed, if that's what you mean. Creative? Yes. Freud tells us that all babies are creative. Practical? Well, I'm still breathing but I believe that walls should be painted by decorators and windows cleaned by window cleaners. Intellectual? As an ox.

Two other things that strike me as a little odd are, first, that there's no mention of sex. It still takes place I'm told and, come to think of it, I hope it's like riding a bike. You'd be odd to want to date and meet someone through Dateline who wasn't in a possible legover situation, I should have thought. I mean, it is in the back of one's mind occasionally. The other odd thing is the question about whether one is interested in conversation. Do they mean that there is any possibility that you *couldn't* be? Have they got mates lined up for

Jake La Motta, the Raging Bull, middleweight champion in 1949.

us who've had their tongues cut out? Perhaps they've got the charwoman of the British Museum Reading Room on their books and are trying to shift her. What Dateline should do is to differentiate between conversation and anecdote and so, I'm afraid, should many pub acquaintances of mine. In fact, as the excellent poet and gentleman George Barker once told me, 'Anecdote is not a form of conversation.' (A sign should be so printed and hung on the wall of every pub in England.)

No, I shan't fill in the form, I'll simply wait and hope to bump into the stranger who'll laugh at my jokes and worship the ground I walk on, as the man said.

Titbits

I don't know why, but recently I've been wondering what on earth it must feel like to be a guide dog. I don't much like dogs but I do love labradors. They're the only dogs that are kind, soppy, forgiving and kind to children. I'd willingly guide a blind labrador. I had one once – a bitch – I called her Smedley and she was pretty extraordinary. One day – during a period when I was desperately skint – she ate an entire weekend's shopping when my back was turned. A shoulder of lamb, some chops, six herrings, the lot – you name it. I kicked hell out of her and she merely retreated to a corner and gazed at me with adoration, wagging her tail ever so tentatively and slowly. You could half kill a dog like that but it'd still love you.

But what of fish? I'm thinking of getting a fish tank and stuffing its waters with inscrutable, flat, slow-thinking things from the oriental deep. If my abode were bigger I'd get a soothing hippopotamus. Looking at them, like looking at Denis Healey, Clement Freud and Kenneth Muir, one is assured that, in spite of being up to here in shit, there's really no *hurry*. Another fancy of mine is for a bird cage. A budgie like Bernard Levin, a vulture like Enoch Powell and a canary like Mrs Thatcher. And what of ferrets like Peter Shore? Put him down a hole and he'd come up with next Sunday's lunch. Then of course there's the taxidermist-defying Cyril Smith. Badger from *The Wind in the Willows*? Not half nice enough. Moby Dick? Too pale. Shirley Williams? A poodle.

This, of course, brings me to just how you'd cook people given your Andes-air-crash-and-subsequent-starvation situation. The recipe isn't the only problem, there's also the matter of where and what part of the anatomy you'd start at. Malcolm Muggeridge is a very slender shish kebab, whereas his disciple, Richard Ingrams, the black-and-white man of television, is simply a piece of burned toast. Martin Amis and Claire Tomalin are olives. Our old friend Alan Watkins boiled beef and carrots.

And what of closer to home? What of that silly game of naming all sorts of things whereby your companion has to guess who the hell you're referring to? In all honesty, picking myself, I find it a real putdown. I know I'm shepherd's pie, a second-hand paperback, a pair of grey flannel trousers, a 1950 Austin Cambridge, a two-mile handicap hurdler, a Kleenex, a paper-clip, an unsharpened pencil (HB2), and an unsolicited advertisement shoved through and up my own letterbox, but at least I'm a large vodka, lime, ice and soda and deserve grilling, marinating and serving hot.

And what about our dear contributors? How on earth do you prepare, cook and serve the likes of Bron Waugh, a man who suffers fools *less* gladly than anyone I know. I think he'd have to be garnished with capers, whereas Ingrams should be pickled. Our editor should be covered in a benign cream sauce and the readers who send letters flambéed. (Ladies, of course may be slightly more nourishing. A shoulder of Antonia Fraser. Spare ribs of Jill Tweedie.) Should the granaries of the world run out, get blown up or go bad, we've always got each other. Meanwhile, I lick my lips and heave in contemplation of the passable feast involving Loren and Wedgwood Benn. May my plane never crash in the Andes or anywhere.

Within limits

The Middlesex Hospital,
Mortimer Street,
London W1

H.M. Prison,
Stanford Hill,
Sheerness, Kent

Dear Ken: Isn't it just typical that both you and I should be in open prisons during Royal Ascot week? Perhaps we should confine our sinning to the winter months, although, as far as you're concerned, conditions would be a little sharper than they would be for me. Eva told me she'd been to see you and that you *seemed* to be bearing up. I take my hat off to you. I'm here for just a few days and already gloom descends only to be lifted by trifling entertainments like eating fairly awful food, ticking off items on the following day's menu and chasing the newspaper man down the corridor as he tries to escape without making a sale. A sadist I shouldn't wonder. But I shouldn't moan to you of all people, banged up as you are in a dormitory full of what might be a very dodgy lot. My cell, as it were, consists of four and my three companions are dead ringers for any and all the other trios I've ever served time with in hospitals. It's a bit like being in rep.

Mr James is the paisley dressing-gown sort and the paisley dressing-gown has usually seen better days. He has silver hair, a clipped military moustache and Tiptree jam on top of his locker and not the cheap stuff. He does the *Daily Telegraph* crossword, usually has trouble with the 'waterworks' and has a rather genteel sort of visitor. He often thinks he's dying but he's as tough as leather. On my left we have Mr Croft who has a pituitary gland disorder which seems to fascinate him as much as it does the medical staff. He's fat, farts a fair amount and is an extremely useful dustbin and waste disposal unit when my friends and visitors bring me excessive amounts of fruit. He's a *Daily Mirror* crossword man and, unlike most tabloid addicts, he's delightfully unsycophantic towards the

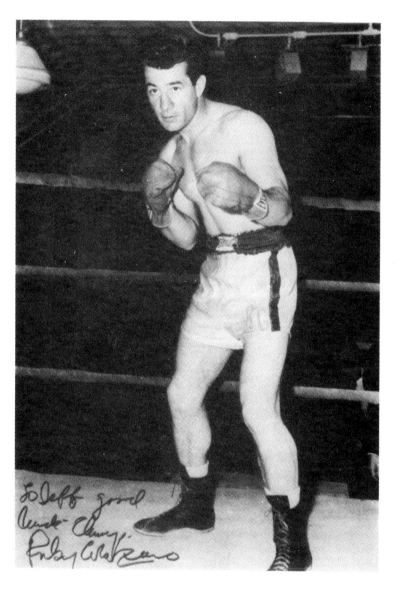

Rocky Graziano. A great middleweight champion in 1947 and still a lovely man.

Middlesex staff. Not a forelock tugger this one. He drinks vast quantities of orangeade and has a strangely musical snore. Last night he changed key at least four times. Very fond of telling the nurses that they're the light of his life.

On my immediate right my fellow sufferer is Mr Jones who absolutely laps up tests of any kind, blood lettings, X-rays and inquisitions from students. The Joneses of the hospital world would be nothing without their illnesses. Diabetes to Jones is what eggs are to bacon. It's just as well for him that the condition is incurable. But he's not daft. He can read a paper, urinate, smoke a cigarette and listen to Radio 2 on his earphones all at the same time and that makes some professional jugglers look a trifle green. Last night he fell asleep with the earphones in and I was tempted to wake him up with a sharp switch over to Radio 3. The funny thing about a lot of Joneses is the way their wives seem proud of them being ill: 'Ooh yes, George has been terribly ill. He nearly died last year, didn't you George? Eight hours they said he had but he's still here, aren't you George?'

As you may imagine, my visitors are slightly different. Norman came to see me yesterday and brought me a vast amount of fruit and cheese. He said I'd been missed that lunch-hour session in the Coach and I said how could I be missed I'd only been in the Middlesex for a few hours. 'Business is business,' he said. And I thought I'd never be loved for my money.

By the way, I gather from your letter to our mutual friend that you are incarcerated with some faily childish nuts and that there was a fracas in your hut over a Mars Bar recently. It's pretty much the same here and we have a daily drama in the day room over what we'll watch on television. Normally and quite rightly it should go by a majority vote, but last night an Irishman flipped when we opted for the news and not an epic about some stolen emeralds dumped in a lake by a villain and safeguarded by piranha fish. The Irishman went quite berserk and called me and Mr Jones some horrible names. Unfortunately for him he's on a drip and it's quite difficult to hit yours truly – slow on his feet this week thanks to various drugs – when you're attached to a stand supporting a bottle of saline solution. Anyway, I had a word with him this morning – a captive audience you might say – and he's been told that we're watching Royal Ascot today come what may, otherwise he'll be in need of medical care. I hope the atmosphere is better in the nick and I hope to see you in time for the Manchester November Handicap.

Yours, Jeff.

Words of wisdom

Dear Bill,

Forgive the familiarity but if we're going to correspond with each other I can't keep addressing you as William, Prince of Wales. Anyway, what prompted me to drop you a line was that pompous balderdash Sir William Rees-Mogg wrote in the *Sunday Times* about your family and implying that you should play the great game of life with a straight bat. Take it from me, old chap, that the difference between a cow shot and an exquisite late cut is simply a matter of timing. I didn't get where I am today with a straight bat.

As to your family and ancestors I must warn you, as one directly descended from Richard Neville, Warwick the Kingmaker, don't count your chickens before they're hatched. Oh, and another warning, if you ever hear your father utter the word Gordonstoun, run for your life. And Bill, talking of life, I always say you only get out of it what you put into it.

Well, I expect you're feeling a little disgruntled, but none of us chooses our parents. Your grandmother is the one to keep an eye on and I advise you to get on the right side of her. I was sick over her tulips under the Royal Box at Ascot in 1971 when I was the *Sporting Life* columnist and you don't see yours truly mentioned in the Birthday Honours List very often. Incidentally, you could take a page out of her book and take up horseracing as a hobby. You get to meet some funny people although her racing manager, Lord Porchester, isn't my idea of a joke; but the bar is open all afternoon.

Sorry, I'm rambling on a bit and all I meant to say was good luck to you. By the way, take a tip from me and stay out of Wales even if you are the Prince of it. They're a horrible bloody lot and God alone knows what your great uncle Ted was doing chatting up those miners. Now he was a card, but more about him when you're a little older. Which brings me to marriage and a word in your shell-like on the subject, if I may, having taken the plunge more times than I care to remember. Your mum and dad are going to try and find you a right one when the time comes to get you a Queen. Hold out, Bill. Don't get stuck with any old bird from Lichtenstein, Schleswig

Holstein, Luxembourg, the Gold Coast or the Falkland Islands. Marry for love, never get anything on the HP and never trust a cabinet.

I do hope this letter doesn't find you as it leaves me. I'm making another appearance in court tomorrow and your granny can detain people at her pleasure and it's a pleasure that can last for 30 years. Thank God you'll never see the inside of a nick. Not unless another Oliver Cromwell emerges from the Fens anyway. Yes, it's not all laughs being a prince or a king. You've got your Charles I getting his redundancy, your Princes in the Tower, Richard II getting his, George III going bonkers, Victoria laying the table for two and, on top of all that, you've got some twit from the *Sunday Times* writing your biography and making a bomb out of it.

Mind you, there are compensations. You've got nice accommodation and I can vouch for the shooting at Sandringham, having bagged a pheasant there one night in '69. You won't go short of a few bob and you'll be able to get away at weekends. I suppose you'll have to go into the navy, cut ribbons and open bridges, plant trees on new housing estates, stand on balconies and wave to American tourists, but at the end of the day you'll be able to put your feet up and decree the odd nightcap or two.

So there we are. We drank your health in the Coach & Horses last week – all week to be truthful – and although Norman is a bit choked that you're not Jewish he sends his regards. As for the bloke who said 'Put not your trust in princes', he didn't know you, did he Bill?

Well, I'll say cheerio now and remain your subjective subject, Jeff.

Half measures

I'm getting a little sick of Soho. There was a time when you could always find somebody there to talk to – your actual conversation I mean – but recently it's been all World Cup and, for longer than that, money. It's really awful how money and the wretched subject of the cost of living have become the main talking points not just in Soho but everywhere. Like the man said about having had an unhappy childhood, money is not a fit subject for conversation. What's more it's the ones who are fairly well-lined – staff hacks on national newspapers and advertising people – who do the most moaning about money. The Americans have a phrase for it, 'crying poor', and it's particularly insulting to cry poor to a man who's holding sweet bugger all in his bin. But now there's yet another form of moaning and it appears in print written by journalists who get banged up when they go to report wars. Surely it's part of the job and to be expected; I've a funny feeling that the man who got nicked after chatting to the Queen while sitting on the edge of her bed was from the *Sunday Times* Insight Team.

This one seems destined for Broadmoor. To ask the Queen for a cigarette is rock bottom and it's also being a trifle mean with your expenses. I know that most journalists live on their expenses and bank their salaries but it reeks of meanness and I expect a conversational moan about the cost of living led up to the business of tapping Her Majesty for a fag. Another giveaway was the business of stealing a half bottle of wine. It's the half that appeals to me. I have seen halves being bought by men who think they're actually entertaining some poor woman in a restaurant and I'm damned if I can think of anything less stylish. Perhaps half bottles are kept for the staff. A footman's life is terribly hard. It's also ludicrous to assume that the Queen smokes in bed. To nod off while re-reading *Black Beauty* and set that lot on fire would be a major disaster, although experts tell me that heat can improve wine. (A wine merchants in Dean Street was hit by incendiary bombs during the Blitz and apparently it performed miracles for what was saved from the cellar.) And where was the Duke. Raiding the fridge?

No it must have been a very nasty experience all round and I'm no stranger to being asked for cigarettes by people when I'm lying in my bed. Usually what's happened is that I've jumped the gun by getting into bed thinking I'd be followed. But what these ladies do is light up a cigarette and then give you a hundred specious reasons for having to go home. 'My husband may phone from Paris.' 'My cat can't bear to be left alone.' 'But we've only known each other for a day.' 'Listen, I like you. I really do, but not like that.' 'The baby sitter will go mad if I'm late.' Sadly I've never had a footman to summon and have these people thrown out before they smoke all my cigarettes. I resign myself to the situation, take a Valium and then fall asleep and burn the bedspread with the last fag. I now have a fire extinguisher by my bed but I never really know whether to aim it at my privates, the lady or the bedspread.

But, skint as I am, I wouldn't give house-room to a half bottle of anything. And now I'm off to Kingsclere for a ten-week ·rest from Buckingham Palace perils and World Cup post mortems, but I fear they'll be discussing the cost of living in the local where I may pop in for the entire full-size bottle occasionally. I shall be reporting to you on the subject of the countryside in July, herbaceous borders, cuckoo spit, possible fairies at the bottom of the *Guardian* and with luck someone beautiful may break into my bedroom and ask me for a cigarette. If it's my favourite clairvoyant I shall give the footman the night off.

Back to nature

Typing, like eating, at a table in a sunshine-filled garden is nearly always impracticable. I am blinded by the whiteness of the paper, and wind rips the bottom half of it back into the keys and there is always a wasp lurking behind me, like a sadistic schoolmaster, wanting to see what I've written. I eat my lunch by the herbaceous border and am joined by every insect in Kingsclere. The merest of breezes cools that which should be hot, before the first bite. My Earl Grey tea is cold before I take the first sip and the bluebottle swimming on the surface is living proof of it. In desperation I switch to vodka and the ice melts away as quickly as a man you've helped. Hacks should work in smoke-filled unventilated rooms, beneath an Anglepoise. Even the charm of the rustic soundtrack begins to grate. The church bells, at first reminiscent of *the* Elegy and all that, go on for just that bit too long and the vicar next door has been giving his lawn a short back and sides for three hours and the motor mower begins to sound like one of those wretched motorbikes in London ridden by psychopathic messenger boys.

But of course it is all very lovely. The only nagging in my mind is that the friends I'm caretaking and cat-sitting for – they're gorging themselves on *fruits de mer* in and around Honfleur – should return unexpectedly and catch me with a dirty ashtray. Consequently I leap from garden to house every five minutes to wipe a surface or wash up a cup and glass. Apart from Great Portland Street not being outside the bedroom window, another bonus is the Crown in Kingsclere. It has just about the best pub food I've come across. Unfortunately, a

In Soho in 1951. Photographed by Pete Arthy.

recommendation from the likes of Egon Ronay and not me tends to fill a place with tourists, or passing trade as they are called. But the landlord's heart is in the right place and I go there every day to unwind. Actually, I don't, and I don't understand that phrase. I drink to wind *up*.

Between the Crown and writing to you, dear reader, my other work is making splendid and rapid progress. I speak, of course, of my long-awaited autobiography. Last week, when I arrived, I wrote my name at the top left-hand corner of a piece of paper and the very next day I wrote the figure '1' opposite. Sometimes my grim determination frightens me. Luckily I have enough self-discipline to stop when all work and no play makes Jack a dull boy and I took myself to Newbury races last Saturday to have another look at the human race. I took my brand new binoculars with me – Russian-made, excellent and extraordinarily cheap – and beheld strange things through them. First, a measure poured out by the racing caterers, Ring & Brymer, and secondly the wintry smile of experience on my ex-wife's face, easily the most attractive face there. She's got a new gimmick now. She keeps brushing non-existent dandruff from my shoulders. This is one of the best and simplest put-downs I know of. The other is to say to someone of me within my earshot, 'He's very sweet *really*'. It's the emphasis on the word 'really' that gets me; you might just as well say it to console a postman who has just had his leg bitten off by your Doberman. But it was nice to back a couple of winners after an excellent picnic, even though all or most of the good 'faces' like Peter Walwyn were away at Keeneland in the USA for the sales.

And now it's back to the grindstone, although the vicar has just decided to hoover the inside of his car. Twixt autobiographical paragraphs of tear-jerking sensitivity and sips of vodka and warm ice I have to write a piece for a women's magazine on 'Women in Pubs'. At least it's something I know about. But how on earth can I concentrate on anything in view of the recent events at this journal in Doughty Street? Next week I shall reveal how the *Spectator* was rocked to its very foundations when security staff discovered that No. 56 is full of heterosexuals. Expect heads to roll. I could kick myself for Mimi (500 old francs, Montparnasse, 1949). How did they find out?

Room to improve

Since Angela Levin of the *Observer* magazine has studiously avoided writing of my one and only favourite room, preferring as she does the old-world charm of Judi Dench's pad and the copper-warming-pan horror of Jean Rook's place, not to mention the ample loot apparent in both, I shall take it upon myself to give you a guided tour of the cell I scream myself to work and sleep in. (Sorry to trouble you but I need to record it as it is now for future reference.) Yes, the memory banks have blown a fuse and framed pictures and collages on the wall are standing in. But the first thing that might strike a visitor to this dark brown study is that it smells like the John Player factory. The window's been open since the beginning of June but we stink of smoke. My best friend, a Dutch cheese plant, thrives on it strangely, but I expect Nelson, whose bust stands on the window ledge, to cough at any moment.

What does appal me is the sundry crap that one collects and ends up surrounded by over the years. I have some unbelievable books – review copies plus unsolicited nonsense from publishers wanting a plug. But I think Miss Levin would want me photographed at my desk. It used to belong to my old and sadly departed friend Frank Norman. He wrote 'Fings Aint Wot They Used T'Be' at it, but, since I acquired it, it has seen no hits. On it at this moment are two summonses from Newbury County Court – hangovers from Lambourn days – a ticking off from the Barclaycard people, a passport that's simply dying to be used, a corkscrew, an overflowing ash tray, a Jockey Club press badge, Valium and a tear jerker of a diary circa 1979. There are six drawers in the desk, one full of determinedly virginal paper, and there's another drawer where the buff nasties go and which is never looked into. By the side of the desk there's a three-litre bottle of Smirnoff that I got on my birthday, which is now collecting 20p pieces. (It took £15 just to cover the bottom of it and when it's full it's the Aegean for me.)

But those pictures on the wall; what a strange assortment. I have to admit that I'm in most of them, but what's Francis Bacon doing with Rocky Graziano, Tom Baker, Lester Piggott, Richard Ingrams,

Tony Zale, Frank Norman, my last three wives, my mum and dad, my brothers, daughter and my prep school cricket team? There's hundreds more but that school team picture somehow embarrasses me now. We look more like a masturbating team than a cricket one and probably were. By my bed, and this is not a suitable journal to discuss that old thing in, there's a fridge. Very comforting in the summer. That contains my favourite glass, vodka, lime, Perrier water, swizzle sticks and orange sorbet. I once found a slice of quiche in it too.

But I'm going to have to clear out a load of books and bung them to Oxfam. If they distribute them carefully I expect *The Alcoholic and the Help He Needs, Florence Nightingale* and *Clever Betting at Your Betshop* will be queued up for in French Equatorial Africa. Other books which might raise a giggle in the jungle are Juliet Mitchell's *Psychoanalysis and Feminism, Depression* – I've a library on that subject – and *Rule Britannia.*

Now the thing is, would I change my chambers in the unlikely event of a pools win or a lunatic legacy? I'd probably consider a penthouse flat overlooking the park and near the Ritz, but I'd have second thoughts. After all, I am semi-retired. Some might say completely so. What more does a man need other than a bed, fridge, bath, a telephone that's mysteriously stopped taking incoming calls from women, an exhausted Barclaycard, a friendly houseplant, fifteen ashtrays and a tolerant landlady? Copper bedwarming pan? Horse brasses? Not on your Nelly. But I do wish Angela Levin would pop round for a drop of the Earl Grey. The chaos here would be a sight for her sore old eyes.

Men's page

If any of you men out there have got any problems you'd like to discuss with me please feel free to write. It's high time someone got a men's page going, and I must assume that the editors of national newspapers have never heard of the Sex Discrimination Act. Last Sunday I spent most of the morning reading a piece about ovarian cysts in the *Observer*. It grabbed me so much that my own cyst-free egg got quite cold alongside the toast. Now don't worry that I'm

My brother Oliver. Photographed by John Deakin *c.* 1952.

going to write about my testicles in a sort of retaliatory way because I'm not, and anyway they still haven't returned to me. But I'm sure you get my drift. I mean why can't they devote a little space to subjects such as 'husband-battering'? And what about beauty care? Every time I look into a mirror I curse the fact that they don't make cosmetics for men. The wear and tear inflicted on one by day-to-day existence is colossal and it shows. Yes, a few beauty tips – and I for one would like to know where Bernard Levin goes to get his hair waved.

I sometimes think these female hacks think that only women have sexual problems. (When you see some of them you realise that premature ejaculation could be a blessing in disguise and I'm pleased to say that Cosmo Landesman is writing a book on the subject.) Yes, they're all so absorbed with their own problems that they can't be bothered to help us find the *male* multiple orgasm. I'd very much like to know just where the hell that's been hiding all these years. It would kill the man who found it, but where's the spirit of Dunkirk? Which reminds me: all the medical advice columns in print are for women only. There's no doctor I can write to to ask why my hands shake, why I forget my own telephone number and why the bed keeps catching fire. And, speaking as an orphan and bachelor, where is there a word of cheer? Women think that only women get depressed and lonely, and as I write this, the tears streaming down the channels of my face, it occurs to me that if I don't get laid this weekend then I may have to make a cry for help. Probably in the Man in the Moon.

There's also very little advice in print for men with career problems. My own is that, quite simply, I'm virtually unemployable, and it's no joke, although I sometimes manage to put on a brave grin. I mean, what the hell can I do? I'm too old and weak now to do anything strictly physical like dig holes and if I got a job as a bank clerk I'd probably get a bit fidgety round about 11 a.m. I couldn't even get a job as a barman since it's assumed that anyone over 40 is on the fiddle. Both Oxford and Cambridge Universities have rejected my proposal to inaugurate a chair of cracker-barrel philosophy and that would have suited me down to the ground. I must admit that the press does indulge in a bit of male fashion, but once a man's got a pair of jeans and jersey, a suit for the races, what on earth more can he want?

My dear friend Irma Kurtz was willing for me to take over her agony column in *Cosmopolitan* for the duration of her holiday but they won't hear of it. You see, they think men can't feel agony. God almighty, if they knew what it was like to have a menopause that lasted 20 years, to have cold flushes and morning sickness for 20 bloody years and to be under the moon every night! And what about those endless interviews they do in women's magazines on the likes of Robert Redford? I don't give a toss for Robert Redford but I'd very much like to know for example whether or not Cyd Charisse has got varicose veins after all these years. Yes, we men must counter-attack the 'women's page' and do the opposite; namely, alienate men from women. The only danger though is that we could end up as a nation of wankers and the trade union movement would never allow that.

Rambling

Help! Help! I'm drowning in memorabilia. I want to jump into tomorrow but how big is the drop the other side of midnight? I'm sorry to go on about my wretched possessions but they've become an obsession and I might go mad if I don't get this room cleared up shortly. Everything I approach, every book, photograph and scrap of paper I want to throw away holds up its arms and screams 'Wait, remember me?' and we sit down together and talk of past times. In desperation I asked my last wife to help me clear out the rubbish this week and she said, 'No. Old wedding pictures depress me as much as they do you.' Quite. Say no more. But you can't throw one away, can you? What about the other people in the picture? It takes an hour to go through such a snap. I wonder where Susannah is now. Seven years ago she spent £40 on a pair of knickers from Liberty. And there's our witness, Charles St George. To think he owned such cracking horses as Bruni, Giacometti and Ginevra and what about the party he gave us at Epsom on the day Shirley Heights won. Of course I'm cutting a lot of short stories short, but you see why I'm stuck in this treacle mire of times past.

There you – or at least I – go again. How did that biography of Edith Piaf get to be on the mantelshelf and why haven't I returned it to John Le Mesurier who lent it me in hospital ages ago? Good old John. I spent two of the nicest days I've ever had with him. One in

Devon chez Dan Farson and one in Newmarket at Teddy Lambton's house and yard. John Le Mes, as he's called, introduced me to Tony Hancock and what a momumental piss-up that turned out to be. Hancock and I started out at opening time in the French pub and I saw him off ten hours later. I put him into a taxi – the driver wouldn't have taken him if he hadn't been Hancock – and he collapsed on to the floor and then handed me his card from a supine position saying, 'Phone me if you get into trouble. I think you may have a drinking problem.'

Which reminds me, what a pity John Le Mes and I never got around to writing the Dictionary of Clichés we planned that weekend with Dan Farson. Come to think of it what a pity Dan doesn't come up to town more often. Such a good and jolly companion and what a twit I must have been twenty years ago to borrow his Pembroke College scarf in an effort to impress a bird in the Duke of Wellington that I was an undergraduate. Now there's a pub that's gone right off. Christ almighty. That's where Dennis Shaw told me that Kennedy had been assassinated. But they did very good scotch eggs in the Wellington. Gilbert Wood used to buy me halves of bitter there when he was painting scenery and when I was an assistant in the cutting rooms at MGM. What the hell was that film called?

God, what a bore that was working in the cutting rooms. *The Guns of Navarone* wasn't too bad though, what with those sessions in the old house at Shepperton Studios. Yes, Gregory Peck took the day off to fly to Rome and back just to see Herb Elliott run in the 5,000 metres. And what was that other race? Oh yes, Chataway *v* Kuts. I watched that in the Swiss pub with George Barker and we won 10/- each. What would that be – 10/-? Just over five pints of bitter I suppose. Pity you couldn't have stuck to bitter isn't it. When on earth was it you – I mean I – first went on the whisky? It must have been 1962 touring *Expresso Bongo* with Mick Tobin as chippy. How I got those flies cues right at the Royal in Newcastle, pissed as a pudding, God alone knows. Married to Jacki then and there's that John Deakin photo of her. When poor old Deakin died in Brighton Francis Bacon went to identify the body and said, 'That's the first time I've seen him with his mouth closed.' Yes, I must return that Piaf book John Le Mes.

Steamy weather

Ever since Russell Square and Jermyn Street ran out of steam I've despaired of ever getting a Turkish bath again. I much prefer them to saunas, which I find claustrophobic and akin to a punishment box in which you sweat it out metaphorically, so to speak, as well as physically. The Turkish bath is, by comparison, spacious. It's also nicely social. You can walk about and have a chat and all sorts of odd balls loom up in the steam. To my surprise and delight our friendly *Spectator* publican, Dave, introduced me to a steam bath just the other day; it must be one of the very few left in this clapped-out city (name and address withheld for fear of tourist invasion). But what a pleasant afternoon I had and in the best of company. As soon as I'd undressed and left the locker room I was introduced to some very stalwart men who were lolling about and melting in the steam room. 'This is Jeff. I'd like you to meet Freddie. Freddie's one of the most successful bank robbers in the country. This is Jim. Jim's just come out after a seven stretch and here's Tom. He's got a spieler in the Commercial Road.' What a jolly bunch they were and the only one who wasn't smiling was Solly, a 70-year-old taxi driver, who was staring mournfully at his prick and intoning: 'We were born together. We grew up together. We got married together. Why, oh why, did you have to die before me?'

The surprise of the afternoon was the picnic they produced in the locker room. Ice-cold lager, vodka, cold chicken, grouse or what you would and then back to the steam and in and out of the cold plunge. After that, a fairly ancient man with fingers of steel gave me an excellent massage which really toned up the cupboard I live in. Just as I was about to get off the slab he surprised me by pouring shampoo on my nut and giving my scalp a massage. Then he hosed me down. I haven't felt so good since Emprerey won the Derby. In fact I felt five years younger, which brought me down to about 70. I think I'll go regularly from now on, and for all that it's a snip for a fiver. It's also quite safe for me to visit Turkish baths now that I've lost my looks. In my pugilistic days, in the days when I could look a clock that was saying 11 o'clock in the face without breaking into a brisk trot to the nearest pub then I had to repel quite a few would-be boarders. Yes, the sign of being over the hill isn't policemen getting younger as far as I'm concerned, it's not being bought drinks by rich queens; the last time someone tried to drown me on the strength of my being a pretty face must be twenty years ago. The journey to the grave is studded with injuries to one's vanity.

Yes, for my money – and that's a joke – the Turkish variety beats the Swedish one hands down. And saunas can be dangerous. A very well-known friend of mine (name withheld, birds still pining, address Heaven) got into the habit of indulging in sexual intercourse in a sauna in a private house. I caught him at it one day and showed him the yellow card, but he would persist. Ten days later he had a heart attack and dropped dead in the street. Sex at 100 degrees and more Fahrenheit just isn't on and it's a pity, considering the climates of their respective countries, that Khomeini, Amin and Gaddafi don't screw themselves to death.

But there'll never be another Jermyn Street. When the jockeys used to use it to take off pounds after the races and after a session in Jules Bar then that was a night on the tiles. And the stories you heard, never mind the tips. But the Russell Square establishment was the best one for a night's kip, which is exactly what I used it for when I was on the bum. At 10 shillings a night it was the cheapest hotel in London and I was the cleanest man in London. And, as I said, I was pretty good at getting ten bobs in those days. Next week's steam bath will have to be paid for by the sweat of this old brow.

Language

Last Saturday I went to Newbury for the races and there was a nice little to do on the train with a ticket inspector. I'd bought a race-train 'special' ticket but jumped aboard an Inter-City when I heard it was going to make a hitherto unscheduled stop at Newbury Racecourse itself. Just before we arrived, this extraordinary ticket collector came into my carriage to do his business. He was real Waffen SS material. About 6ft 6ins, severe-looking with a pencil moustache and wearing an impeccably pressed Germanic BR uniform, he wasn't one to take prisoners, I could see. I was sitting in a first-class compartment and

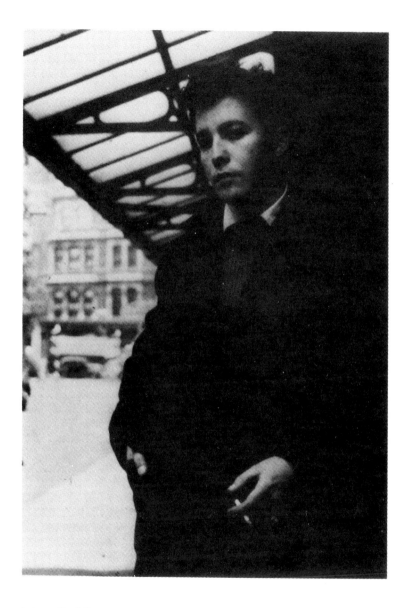

A juvenile delinquent posing outside the Palace Theatre for John Deakin, 1953.

had to give him the excess fare. But the bastard made me pay the entire fare again because he said special race-train tickets couldn't be transferred to other trains. This peeved me somewhat, as did his officious manner. I remarked, with some sarcasm, seeing how he relished the incident, 'I suppose you really enjoy your job.' Drawing himself up to a good 6ft 7ins he replied, 'Yes sir, I do. And, furthermore, I was created and not born, sir.' I'd be extremely grateful to any reader who can tell me what on earth that might possibly mean.

At the time words failed me, except for the short one which always springs to mind. I barked it out and a 16-year-old boy in the corner of the compartment busy taking down railway engine numbers turned scarlet and seemed on the verge of a fit. (However boring swearing may be I'm suspicious of people who are squeamish about it.) I was feeling very irritated by now and was tempted to turn on the boy to tell him that if he spent more time abusing himself and others his spots would clear up in no time. Then at Reading we were joined by a man who was carrying a copy of the *Sun* and was covered in tattoos. By Newbury I was feeling sick. The idiot inspector who drew himself up to his full height every time he opened his mouth, the boy a physical wreck at the mention of an obscene word and a tattooed *Sun* worshipper. What were they trying to tell us? Not for the first time I reflected that Desmond Morris's Body Language is only the half of it. These gestures bear closer examination.

I often wonder about a girl who works on a newspaper I go to, whose every physical movement and gesture is pure posture. You probably know the type. They sit on the floor a lot and, if they're wearing jeans, they wave their legs about. When they stand and talk their arms point and wave like so many Isadora Duncan contortions. They smoke cigarettes *professionally*. The smoke is inhaled very sharply and the teeth are bared. Then the head turns to give you a profile and the smoke is exhaled slowly and deliberately and the grey jet stream becomes a beautiful blue cloud of smoke. What are they trying to tell us? Well, all that, like compulsive face-pulling, is simply a sign of pure, stark terror. Such women also have their disgusting equivalent of the male tattoo; that is, they wear their sunglasses on top of their heads. This is to indicate that they are racy, with it and a cut above a shop girl.

But it's 'Fat' Tom's body language that fascinates me most. About once a month in the Colony Room Club you can see him sitting upright on his bar stool swigging away, when suddenly but slowly the stool starts to tilt backwards and Tom descibes the perfect arc of 90 degrees and crashes full length on to the floor. What is Tom trying to tell us? It's hard to say. I've examined him closely when he has come to rest on the floor, but I've never been able to get a flicker of recognition out of him.

To come back to the sunglasses on the top of the head, it did ring a bell when I read in *The Human Zoo*: 'Female monkeys in captivity have been seen to offer themselves sexually to a male as a means of obtaining food morsels ...' Ah yes, all those dinners in Wheeler's in the good old days.

Downcast

One afternoon last week I lost a £50 note. The same evening I had a carrier bag containing a brand new sweater stolen from the French pub. This morning I received a buff-enveloped rebuke from Barclaycard. I went into the kitchen to read it and as I did so I dropped a piece of toast and marmalade on to the floor and it landed face down. The loss of the £50 note infuriated me and left me with just a quid but the toast landing marmalade-down has really depressed me and I feel I can no longer remain an atheist. There can be no doubt that there is somebody up there and they hold me in the greatest contempt. I shall leave my flat later this morning carrying a white flag. I give up. D'you know, the toast and marmalade has *always* landed face down. It has to be symptomatic of something. Cliché-mongers keep telling me that 'something will turn up' so why can't it be the toast and marmalade? It may all sound frightfully trivial to you but, you see, it's the thin end of the wedge of which a slightly thicker section is having lost at least 12lbs while waiting for a cheque from the *Daily Telegraph*.

There is one consolation, though; I can't stop laughing, albeit inwardly. Most blessings are heavily disguised. Apart from the fact that I'm not allowed to eat marmalade anyway, I vaguely remember having left a chunk of cod fillet in the carrier bag with the sweater and by this time the thief will have come to acknowledge that it is better to give than to receive. And when I think of the men that women have left for me then I can barely repress a chuckle. I remember once being given a severance kiss in favour of a property dealer who turned out to be impotent. There was also a woman in Marylebone who, having recited to me the famous soliloquy 'You Make Me Sick', jumped into her car and drove straight into a wall, blinded no doubt by crocodile tears.

But all that's behind me now and there'll be less marmalade face-down, so to speak, now that I've decided to give up the pursuit of women. Until now I've never been anti-blood sports but at last the chase has begun to sicken me. It's so incredibly undignified for one thing, and it's an elementary fact that if somebody doesn't reciprocate then they're simply the wrong person. What one needs is a load of self-protective arrogance. Only recently – my very last metaphorical marmalade incident I hope – I became pretty interested in a very obvious-looking woman; that's to say a well-packaged one. I offered to make her extremely unhappy, but she preferred one of the ghastliest and ugliest men in Soho, whom she thought to be 'steady' and 'reliable' since he dabbles in publishing, whatever that is. In fact the man's as shallow as a single scotch but he can wag a wallet as well as his tail. Now I'm very well aware of the fact that the easiest way to drive a woman into a man's arms is to knock him behind his back, so I did the reverse. I told her that the creep was good, kind, talented and a candidate for heaven. This was pretty nasty of me. For the next twenty years she'll be scraping the toast every morning and he'll be dropping it marmalade-side-down. Buttering a man up can occasionally mesmerise a woman but, as I say, the reverse is usually true, and since I'm supposed to be 'difficult' and 'wicked' according to my Soho press agent I can't understand why some nice woman isn't knocking on my door. Some shit has obviously been saying nice things about me. Yes, it's been a lousy week and Puccini hasn't helped much. With him being composer of the week I've spent every morning crying from 9 a.m. to 10 a.m. When Mimi drops the toast marmalade-side-down it breaks my heart.

All abroad

My French stinks. It seems that when I asked somebody for a light I asked them to set me on fire and when I asked the concierge for an

One of John Deakin's best pictures: brother Bruce, Terry Jones and me outside the Mandrake Club about 1954.

alarm call I apparently asked him to wash me at 6 a.m. Never mind. Their English stinks too. I got caned at school for reading a novel during a French lesson and the memory of it was pretty sharp in Paris last weekend where I went to see the Trusthouse Forte-sponsored Prix de l'Arc de Triomphe. Personally, I wouldn't have trusted Trusthouse Forte to sponsor a cup of tea but it was a great race and God knows the Aga Khan needs the £168,000 prize money. Anyway, the weekend kicked off with a freebie trip to Boulogne sponsored by P&O Ferries and they and the Boulogne Chamber of Commerce laid on a champagne breakfast on the boat and then your slap-up lunch in the town itself. I don't really get it. Can my mentioning P&O get them any more business? And what of the other hacks in the party? With the exception of my friend and agony auntie Irma Kurtz they were, as hacks tend to be, pretty bloody ghastly. But, what with giving Irma the loan of my ears and being unable to keep my eyes averted from the amazing legs of a very jolly PR lady called Judy Carter, I managed to avoid them. Press trips usually contain 90 per cent bores, although Hazel Evans once pushed me into a moat surrounding a chateau in the Loire valley which was very refreshing.

Now the lunch was really good, and between Irma telling me about the meaning of life and telling me to give up sex because it's over-rated I did manage to eat some crab, prawns, langoustine, moules marinière, boeuf bourguignon, coq au vin and ice cream. Oh yes, and a glass of wine as well. Drinking is one hell of a problem in France for me since vodka's too expensive there and it's the only drink that doesn't make the pancreas scream. After lunch I lounged around a few bars sipping pastis and watching the English at play. What on earth is it that turns an Englishman into a Manchester United supporter as soon as he crosses the Channel? I saw one lout actually whistle at a waiter to gain his attention and afterwards I felt compelled, albeit somewhat pompously, to apologise to the patron for my own race.

After watching the idiots kicking beer cans in the street I retired to Wimereux and the Hôtel du Centre which advertises itself as having an 'ambience sympathique'. It's funny how the French go on about being sympatico but I suppose we all have our silly fantasies. A good hotel though, and to bed with a veal escalope. Incidentally, although I ate very well in France by my standards, things were slightly spoilt by an odd compulsion to wonder, 'Now, would Bernard Levin eat this?' every time I sat down to munch. I suppose an obscene article he once wrote about food still hasn't been digested by my mind.

The following day I caught the train to Paris and was reminded for the thousandth time how awful British Rail is. Saturday was a scorcher. I walked for miles, got back to my hotel, filled the bidet with cold water and stood in it for ten minutes to cool off the feet. I'd watched the rich at play in and around the Champs Elysées and, by God, they really are pretty revolting. They're so bloody posh and they never stop play-acting at being stars. If the Prince de Galles is the high life then give me the gutter. A man shouldn't have to *wear* his money. One lovely sight though, and that was the food shops in the Rue des Martyrs. But even the French are having an attack of the hamburgers and there was a Wimpy next to my hotel near the Gare du Nord.

Came Sunday and the Arc de Triomphe. I'd seen two before only. In 1970 my first column for the *Sporting Life* concerned the Arc when Sassafras beat Nijinsky by a head. That day I got involved with a couple of Irish trainers and we were still at the paddock bar as the moon came up. A year later I was back to see Mill Reef win. I won £50 on the race and moments after I'd collected it someone walked up to me and said, 'By the way, you've got the sack from the *Life.*' That called for more champagne. This year the French were at their most uncooperative and the men on the gate refused to believe that the Jockey Club had left me a pass. Luckily my old friend Charles St George, who owns Ardross, was nearby and he, of course, marched me in. It seemed something of an omen to me to bump into him first and I was just one of a thousand English people rooting for Ardross.

But what about Longchamp? It lacks the atmosphere of Ascot and it's packed with people who go there to be seen. The office, too, was even more toffee-nosed than I'd remembered and although they did give me a pass they said I couldn't go into the enclosure until after the last race because I wasn't wearing a tie. I was beginning to wish that I was back in the Coach & Horses, and suddenly I was. I walked out of the office and, lo and behold, who should be standing there but 'Bookshop' Billy, 'Big' Tom, Brian 'The Burglar' and 'Irish' Patsy. I could have hugged them. What a sight they were drinking beer in front of the lawn where stands the statue of the first French winner of the Epsom Derby in 1865, Gladiateur, nicknamed 'The Avenger of Waterloo'. We swilled away at the beer and the Soho lads went to back the English-owned-and-trained and Pat Eddery-ridden Sharpo.

He won quite beautifully, and he won about £60,000 and 'un objet d'art' for his owner Monica Sheriffe. Here was ammunition for the Arc and the Soho team stuck it on Ardross for England, and themselves of course. It's history now but the Aga Khan's Akiyda just beat Ardross. Lester rode a great race on Ardross but the horse needs a shade further and, in fact, in 15 races now Ardross has only lost three times and over the Arc distance of a mile and a half. Charles St George and a mite of patriotic fervour apart – I didn't have a bet – I was a little bit choked that the Aga Khan won. Not a nice man and here's not the place to say why. Still, the prize money didn't go to Daniel Wildenstein either, another prize one.

At the end of the afternoon I was in my usual state which is on my uppers. The Soho team took very good care of me though and we retired to a beautiful hotel called the Harlequin for cocktails. After that a very good and expensive dinner, so I'm told, but wasted on me by then. The next morning it was back to Boulogne again to get the ferry. The buffet car on the train this time was first rate. An English woman and her ten-year-old daughter gave me dirty looks all the way because I was drinking pastis. How odd it is that some of us still think it's immoral to drink before official opening time in England. It's also odd that the inventors of chips, the English, seem to make them out of cotton wool. My 'desert island' meal, apart from a bible-and-Shakespeare sandwich, would be that old French standby of steak, pommes frites, salad, cheese and claret.

Today, I'm afraid, it's back to steak pie and two veg in the Coach. It's also back to the likes of Brighton, Uttoxeter, Lingfield and Sedgefield – a far cry from Longchamps, but a cosier one. Yes, it's back to earth, finding the rent and that old spot of skating on thin ice. But you wouldn't want that thin ice to give way in Paris. They'd hold you under. By the way, I'm not talking through my champagne, but P&O are better than Sealink and even the people in Greek Street are better than those damn people in the Champs Elysées.

Country Matters

I went to Suffolk last weekend after ten years. I fled it with tears in my eyes and the return match on Sunday brought tears to my eyes for different reasons. God, what creeps! Of course my old cottage has been done up. You could play billiards on the lawn where I spent summer afternoons with my hand up someone's skirt and they've knocked down the garden shed in which I began the novel of the century – the skirt distracted me after page one – but the twits have torn down the honeysuckle. Most of the village bores are still intact though and the next idiot who tells me to 'always plant your potatoes on Good Friday' is going to have his pint of bitter poured over him. As I explained, through gritted teeth, there are no potatoes in Great Portland Street. Although the Peacock Inn has been done up too I felt as though I'd just popped out for a pee when I walked through the door. The same conversations were still in progress if you can call standing and thinking progress.

Sundays are the days when the middle classes dress down. The men wear old army jerseys full of moth holes, green gumboots, torn trousers – a barrister wears an old court-room striped pair – and the stains of motor mower oil are displayed like Pistol's wounds collected on St Crispin's Day. For the ladies, husky coats are *de rigueur*. Conversation embraces the price of property, jam making, jumble sales and was the vicar pissed this morning. The middle bar is two steps down the social ladder and is packed by the sort of people who indulge in roadside picnics, keep budgerigars and use metal teapots. They all share the same brain. The back bar is for the local working men. All of them can tickle trout, catch pheasants with their bare hands, sell you a car for £5, mend your washing machine for the price of a drink and tell you never to put in tulip bulbs on an odd day of the month when it's raining and the missel-thrush is silent. The likes of me are regarded as dangerous and eccentric. Twelve years ago, the local gentry struck me off the cocktail party circuit because I had a piss in the rectory flower bed – a little recycled Tio Pepe never killed a wallflower, but such things live in their memories. My affair with the vicar's daughter has now assumed Profumo-like proportions – mere dalliance in the organ loft – and legend has it that I used to drink *all day* in Sudbury with Maurice Richardson on market days. I should bloody well hope I did. Dear Maurice.

But there were some new faces. Anybody with a few bob these days puts it into a cottage. The men take up weekend lawn mowing as though it's a career and the women are drawn to crafts. If there's anything more disgusting than art then it's crafts. Making corn dollies is not a suitable pastime for an attractive woman and, by the way, the country is still beautifully untouched by feminism. Furthermore I'll thank country women to clear out the pottery clay from under their fingernails before they caress my magnificent body and I'll thank them too for not cooking everything in sunflower seed oil, attracting flies by nude sunbathing and bringing their peanut butter encrusted children into pubs. Yes, it's odd that. Middle-class children are addicted to peanut butter. I suppose it's an easy way to keep them alive and far cheaper than an oxygen tent.

Sadly, my host was cruelly exposed by his small son at the weekend. His friend asked him 'What does your daddy do?' Jimmy told him, 'He goes to London every day, goes into pubs, cashes cheques and gives the change to mummy.' There's no answer to that, nor should there be.

Off colour

I've known Aubrey since we were teenagers but I never realised until last week that he's a paranoid hypochondriac. Like most of us he's worried about pollution, excessive crop-spraying and the fast-vanishing hedgerow. The general decline of his neck of the woods and fields has got him twitching and the thing that bugs him most is the physical damage that he claims to have suffered in the last year from motor car and lorry exhaust fumes. Now, what he's done is to list his ailments on paper and circulate them to neighbours within a 5-mile radius, and if they too can say they've suffered from any affliction on the list then he wants them to sign a petition asking the government to ban insecticides and cars from the said neck of woods and pastures. I shall allow Aubrey to continue this column now by simply quoting his 1982 health chart. You're not going to believe it, but I promise you this is his circular. This is what one man claims to have suffered from in one little year.

1. Lassitude (*acute* tiredness). 2. Distraction (lack of concentration). 3. Aching (heavy limbs). 4. Bouts of severe depression. 5. Back ache, shoulder ache. 6. Sudden acute pains in rib cage, limbs and extremities. 7. Lengthy headaches. Sudden sharp pains in temples and forehead. 8. Pains on inside of forearms. 9. Cystitis, difficulty and frequency in passing water. 10. Drawing sensation towards lower abdomen. 11. Aching backs of hands as with sprain. 12. Popping, aching, tickling ears. 13. General acute itching. 14. Violent sneezing. 15. Indigestion. Inflated, bloated, acidic. 16. Nausea. 17. Catarrh (not necessarily related to a cold). 18. Sore gum, tongue and inside of mouth with ulcers and cold sores. 19. Sores in nostrils. 20. Sore throats and swollen glands. 21. Bowel trouble – diarrhoea, motions in small quantities of soft consistency. 22. Very sharp hot pains of short duration in rectum.

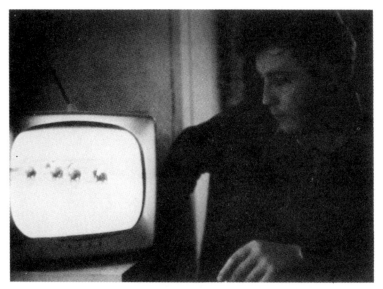

The rot sets in. Watching racing on TV, 1960.

23. Raw stinging circle around anus. 24. Eye trouble – stabbing sensation through eyeballs, pulling, drawing feeling. 25. Watery eyes, itching eyes, dry gritty eyes, itching lids, blurred vision, foggy eyes, winking eyelids. 26. Sweating, not related to exercise. 27. Runny nose. 28. Slurred speech. 29. Bad physical coordination. 30. Bleeding from rectum. 31. Irritability. 32. Dizziness. Loss of balance. 33. Continuous clearing of throat. 34. Bad breath and bad taste in mouth. 35. Heavy lump high in centre of chest. 36. Fluttering in chest. 37. Hormone trouble. 38. Erratic pulse.

Phew! Amazing, isn't it. And I thought I was dying a little too soon. But there are some lovely unconscious touches here and only a serious man could be so unintentionally funny. I particularly like 'sweating, not related to exercise' – the buff envelope with the window syndrome? – and I'm not surprised that 'irritability' follows 'bleeding from rectum' although medically speaking I'm sure he doesn't know his arse from his elbow. But he's obviously taken to drink hasn't he? (I haven't seen him for 10 years.) The slurred speech, stomach pains, bad coordination and loss of balance all point to it and, speaking as a specialist, I'm rather touched to see that he's tried to go on the wagon. 'General acute itching' is merely a withdrawal sympton. The bit about bad breath leads me to suspect his tipple is white wine. People who drink wine without food smell like drains. The heavy lump and fluttering in the chest is what we call angst. As for the bouts of severe depression and acute tiredness one can only suppose that he's embarked on the *Spectator* Treasure Hunt. Why he doesn't go to a hospital God only knows. Perhaps, in spite of being a hypochondriac, he agrees with my friend Eva. She once asked a man in a pub, 'What do you do?' He said, 'I practise medicine.' She said, 'Practise? Why don't you get it right?'

Too much

There hasn't been a lot to laugh about this past week. After thirty years I'm back to 9st, the featherweight limit, and what's more I now need middle-distance glasses to read the bathroom scales. Is a mere 5ft 9ins middle distance? The looking-glass has lost its fascination for me and now, as the trembling razor scrapes along the hangdog valleys of my face, I'm moved to morbid curiosity. When the door-bell rang this morning I was sure it was the grim reaper, but luckily it was the milkman. What worries this incredible shrinking man though is the fact that I've been working on a magazine feature about food and over the last two weeks I've tucked into as much good grub as you or I could want. On top of that, Messrs West and Wheatcroft kindly fed me in the Gay Hussar yesterday – unfortunate name that nowadays – and when Victor suggested the goose he was staring at my neck. Yes, I feel well and truly plucked. Too late, I fear, has come the news that surgeons at Addenbrookes can now play at pancreas transplants. Of course what they should be working on is the cash transplant. Which reminds me, Taki's in town.

Now what else was I going to moan about? Oh yes, the old gripe about staff hacks on £15,000 and more a year who don't know how lucky they are. Get this. A female reporter on the *Daily Mirror* was asking Jilly Cooper about the fact that she was selling her London home and moving to the country. When Jilly said, 'To paraphrase Doctor Johnson, I'm sick of London but not tired of life', the reporter asked, 'Is this Johnson private or National Health?' It's bloody marvellous, isn't it? Here we are, supported only by belt and braces, struggling to make a large vodka last 20 and not 15 minutes, stealing hardboiled eggs from the counter of the Coach & Horses when Norman's not looking, reduced to 50p each way accumulators, humiliated into seducing those who'll do it for a Chinese takeaway, burning our candle at one end and our fingers with dog ends, writing our sexual reminiscences for a soft porn magazine, recycling tea bags, cadging Sunday lunches, going in for newspaper competitions, smashing our piggy banks and we have a professional journalist who's never heard of Doctor Johnson but who can bank her salary and live comfortably off her expenses. Pass the hemlock.

You know, I just don't know what goes on in schools today. Last week I saw my daughter. She's nearly 13 but her reading is slow and her handwriting is laboured. With luck she may suddenly blossom, but I suspect that the priorities at Holland Park Comprehensive School are rolling joints of marijuana and listening to pop. Well, this pop has been asked to get the autograph of one Harrison Ford. Now I don't expect her to ask for Professor A.J. Ayer's autograph but I do hope she's heard of Doctor Johnson by the time she's been deafened by her first disco.

And I'm off to a seat of learning soon. The Cambridge Union want me to do something silly. What I want to know is how the hell they thought to phone me up at the Coach & Horses. There I was, having a quiet drink with a *Daily Mirror* reporter and explaining that Magna Carta was *not* King John's wife and that the Duke of Wellington was *not* a general but a pub in Wardour Street, when this undergraduate homed in on me. You can't give a vodka and history master class without someone getting at you now, and I wouldn't be in the least surprised if God or the devil phoned up next week to ask me to drop dead for some charity or other.

Trial and error

It's been another silly week I'm afraid, and one punctuated with some very strange judgments. On one day, I forget which, a woman who inflicted sixteen cigarette burns on the hand of her baby was sent to prison for six months. On the same day, a man who stole

£25,000 from his firm was sent down for four years. And what is £25,000? Pieces of paper. Then there was the Miss World contest which I think may have been judged by blind eunuchs. Miss Trinidad and Tobago, the one with the Cleopatra-style hair, was head and shoulders above her rivals but came nowhere. But why stop at head and shoulders? And why the hell should the result irritate me so much? God knows, but I know how much the contest irritates some women. It shouldn't. If I had the chance of winning £10,000 by walking across a stage wearing swimming trunks I'd jump at it and I'd thank the men's liberation movement to mind their own business.

Another thing that's subsequently irritated me about Miss World is that she's been boasting in the press that she's a virgin. She says she wants to keep herself pure for her marriage. Quite frankly, I do not wish to know such things of this particular nature. I tried to keep myself pure for my first marriage, too, but fell by the wayside when I met Miss Notting Hill Gate 1947. But that's beside the point and a story I'm saving for *Spare Rib*.

Yes, the judges of the Miss World contest say that 'personality' counts for a hell of a lot. By personality they mean saying – preferably with a Venezualan accent – that you like water skiing, want to start a family, be a model and open your own hairdressing shop. Faced with the same interview, covered in goose-pimples and standing in my swimming trunks on the stage of the Albert Hall, I can see that I'd lose valuable points for saying that I'd like to stop a family and open a beach bar in Barbados with an intact and pure Miss Trinidad and Tobago.

The other judgment which I found odd was the one made against me in court. I've fallen behind with some monthly payments and when I explained to the beak that the reason for this is because I've been a trifle skint, he *upped* the instalments. I can't see the logic of it. The man could get a job with the Arts Council, whose judges always give the money to those who've got enough already. Incidentally, and I'm sure I've said it before, have you noticed how much it helps nowadays to be a little bit black if you're after a grant or a world beauty title? Personally, I don't much mind being discriminated against but what I do object to is the ridiculous business of not being allowed to make jokes about black people or Jews. Sorry, Jewish people. Why you should be immune and the Irish and Polish not, I don't know. I should have thought they too have suffered enough over the years.

One of my heroes, Fred Winter, a great jockey and now trainer, taken in 1965.

Anyway, another crazy thing this week was the invitation that came through the post inviting me to a press conference and buffet lunch given by the British Diabetic Association. God knows how they got hold of my name since I'm not a member, but a diabetic buffet lunch? I ask you. Of course I didn't go. My idea of the lunch hour (*hour*?) does not encompass a plate of bran washed down with whatever we're allowed to drink, and I don't even know what we are allowed to drink. And, apart from Jews and blacks, did you know that it's considered bad taste to make jokes about diabetics. There's too much squeamishness in the world.

Which reminds me, I couldn't help but laugh when I read about the poor sod who'd had a heart transplant and who sadly snuffed it this week. His widow complained that immediately after the operation he became a raving sex maniac. I've never heard of such post-operative spin-offs but I have experienced that same sort of sense of urgency in the middle of the night when I've heard my own heart beating. A shortage of breath confirms the diagnosis that I must now rush out to contact some Smirnoff and Miss Trinidad and Tobago before it's too late.

Scrubbing along

With the passing of time, words change their meaning and, most of all, their feeling. Young people today have got the word 'scrubber' all wrong and Miss Zetterling's film has further distorted the meaning of the word. This is not to knock the film, just the title. Originally, scrubber was a Royal Navy word. A seaman who scrubbed the deck of a ship was doing the lowliest job on board. The word then came to be used to describe a woman in port who was easy to pick up; that is, available. It has never meant prostitute and it has never applied to a woman solely living by crime. It has to do with style. It is NOT necessarily derogatory.

As a general rule scrubbers tend to be rather lonely, a little frightened, untidy, kind, promiscuous, fond of men, vulnerable, brave and a bit of a mess. One clue to a scrubber is the way she treats her knickers. They are often worn for two consecutive days and/or left on the bedroom floor until it's launderette day. By Norman Mailer's account Marilyn Monroe was an extremely unhygienic woman in this respect and she was also one hell of a mess. She was, in fact, the Queen of Scrubbers. But that had nothing to do with blond hair, tits and legs. Mae West was a lady, but Jean Harlow was a scrubber. Madame de Pompadour was a lady, and that lovable, funny, pain-in-the-arse Dorothy Parker was a scrubber. Scrubbers often turn up early for dates with hopeless men whom they try to look after. Sex is emotional currency and a great comfort for the bedsitter girl with ladders in her stockings and mascara on the pillow. She can laugh through her tears though. (Can you imagine Margaret Thatcher crying herself to sleep?) Most scrubbers, like old

78

soldiers, fade away, although they're prone to suicide attempts which go wrong and succeed. They have a very unlucky track record as far as unintentional pregnancies are concerned. Life has them on the ropes but they rarely go down for a count of nine breather.

But, to turn to men, it's to be hoped that if anyone is contemplating a film called Spiv that they get that right too. Spiv was originally an American police acronym for Suspicious Person Itinerant Vagrant. Its wider usage came into being during the austerity years imposed by Stafford Cripps. The Spiv wore gaberdine drape suits with massive shoulder pads, heavily Brylcreemed hair and suede 'brothel creepers'. He bought and sold cars, clothing coupons or anything you found hard to get. Above all, he never had a regular job when work was more of a virtue than the necessity it is now.

He no longer exists. Spiv has taken on a new meaning and here again it's a matter of style and feeling. Today's spiv is a smoothie more than anything. He is to be found in advertising, television, Fleet Street and, by the score, in the House of Commons. Harold Wilson was a spiv, as is David Steel. Andre Previn is a spiv and so are Michael Caine and Michael Parkinson. A friend opines that Melvyn Bragg is one but I'm sure he has occasional moments of self-doubt. Most Soho spivs work at producing television commercials. They gather in the French pub and are compulsive chatters-up of women. (Very boring, that.) Henry V was a spiv but Edward VII was a gentleman. Napoleon was a spiv and Wellington a gentleman.

Spivs like eating in trattorias and they frequent cocktail bars like Stringfellows and discos like Tramp. I suppose that one of the things I like about my pub, the Coach, is that we have hardly a spiv on the premises. Survivors are thick on the ground. We have idiots, bores, hooligans, scallywags, scoundrels and the passing scrubber, thank God, but we're mercifully understaffed when it comes to spivs. What I have got which is odd is the feeling that in a previous incarnation I was a scrubber. Sometimes I could swear I once sat on Edward VII's knee, my lipstick smudged and my knickers at half mast.

In all sincerity

There are very few sights more revolting and disgusting afforded to the owner of a television set than that of a gaggle of actors and actresses freeloading in a common, vulgar Park Lane hotel collecting awards that look like bronze Henry Moore turds and slapping each other on the back and kissing each other on the cheeks with all the sincerity of a psychopath committing perjury in the Number One court of the Old Bailey. What is even more ghastly is the fact that these people have their words put into their mouths by writers. Thespians, by and large, strike me as humanoid puppets suspended and operated by egomaniacs and entrepreneurs like Peter Hall and National Theatre white elephants like any director with a beard and a house in Hampstead. The body language of the self-congratulatory theatre clique is as thick, treacly and sick-making as the treacle and brimstone of Dotheboys Hall. Barry Norman grows his hair over his ears. Why? As the awards are announced, dinner-jacketed, so-called stars clap and laugh at pedestrian speeches, mini-addresses and embarrassed asides as though they were applauding Sheridan, Fox or Churchill. Watching the box last Monday night – I can't even remember the names of the awards or programme – I was reminded of a typical Francis Bacon aside – not the 1561-1626 Bacon – that the only way to survive life, that short interval 'twixt birth and death, is to regard very, very nearly everything as being totally unimportant. Show business, it seems, is terribly important. But I don't not respect just actors, I think the wordsmiths who make them ejaculate are as bad.

Put it another way. Last week, our lovable editor was in the Duke of York and in a good mood. 'Look here, Jeff,' he said, 'I thought your column last week was pretty okay. Have a drink.' Silence descended as Dave Potton assaulted the vodka optic twice before plonking the ice, squeezing the lime and squirting the soda into the crystal goblet. I walked up to the bar – trotted and bounced up to it more like the stars in fact – and turned to address the pub.

I kissed the barmaids on both cheeks and said, 'Thank you, darlings. It's been a great privilege and an honour to receive this drink. I'd like to say that it's been a team effort and I want to thank, not only my wonderful editor, but also Jennifer Paterson without whose motorscooter peregrinations to the Coach & Horses the column would never have arrived at the typesetters; Gina Lewis whose expert subbing prevented the column from being spiked; Jenny Naipaul for phoning me to remind me it was copy day and last, but not least, Sukie Marlowe for giving me an encouraging wink. I'd also like to thank all those people who made me feel sufficiently inadequate to take refuge in journalism – my mother, my headmaster, four wives, bookmaker and Smirnoff. Finally, I'd like to add that I'm sorry Richard West is away in Hong Kong or Huntingdon and I'd like to accept this other vodka on his behalf. Thank you.'

It was a wonderful evening and I shall always treasure the drink that is now on my mantelshelf. It makes me feel so important and it's wonderful to know that we're all truly wonderful.

Eva

Eva Johansen died last week in a typically extravagant, sad and infuriating way: drunk in bed with a cigarette and, like what ever little money she ever had, up in smoke. It's unlike her to be so inconsiderate. Soon there'll be no one left at all to drink with. Melancholy is giving way to a sort of dull anger at being deprived of the pleasure of her company. She once wrote to me, 'It was good to see you the other day. I'd forgotten how much our rows meant to me.' And again last week after I tried to cheer her up, 'Thank you for looking after me; it's so nice to know that you're there between rows.' But it was she, in fact, who looked after me. No wonder I feel so selfish about her death. I too will miss our screaming matches as well as the blissful days.

In spite of having just the one foot on the ground – she was a bit of a romancer at times – she set great store on us both being Gemini and it appealed to her that Marilyn Monroe and Judy Garland both were too. There's no need to remind you of what happened to them. But if there was anyone famous whom Eva put me in mind of it must be Dorothy Parker. Sometimes her unconscious efforts to imitate that lady infuriated me and I'd tell her not to try so hard. That would invariably lead to a slanging match – invariably in a pub – and to an anxious and inquiring landlord. She'd stop swearing at me, smile and say, 'Oh, it's quite all right. This is a friend of mine and I'm simply trying to explain to him that he's a stupid bastard.' Exit puzzled landlord.

Our longest-standing trivial row, which became eventually our longest-standing joke, was about the breakfast she demanded when she was staying with me in the country. I asked her what she wanted and she said, 'I'd like a slice of cold, rare, roast beef and a glass of Tio Pepe, preferably from the fridge.' I said, 'Why can't you have a fucking egg like anyone else, you flash cow?' and she replied, quite rightly, 'Because I'm not anyone else.' And she wasn't.

She was also very deft at putting a man down when she wanted to, although in the end, they put her down with an almighty thump. I remember a creep of a travelling salesman – she picked up the phrase from one of her heroes, Auberon Waugh, and called the type 'these people' – approached her in our local with a view to picking her up and said, 'Good morning. Nice day.' She gave him a look of utter disdain and said, 'Your place or mine?' Exit frightened rabbit. But if there is anything to astrology and her obsession about Gemini then it is borne out by the two faces that were Eva. Inside the abrasive, tough, hard-drinking woman there was a frightened little girl trying desperately *not* to get out. Well, she got out last week.

I shall miss the asides as well as her company. A very good friend of hers was once foolhardy enough to tell her, 'You know, Eva, if I hadn't met you I think I would have taken up keeping bees.' He was ever after referred to as 'The Bee Keeper' and she said, 'The poor sod wanted to keep bees and he ended up with a hornet's nest.' But let her finish this column with an excerpt from a typical letter she wrote three years ago.

'So I have no flat, no job, no lover, no income and – as far as I can see – no prospects. Even my cat has left me. I keep sitting around expecting fear and all I'm getting is exhilaration ... So here I am exulting in the clean dry air of absolute selfishness, secure in the knowledge that there is nothing more they can do to me. If it weren't so totally out of keeping with everything I've been told, I'd say it could only be described as happiness.'

With Frank Norman in Soho, 1970.

Out of the mouths

If the age of consent was raised from 16 to 50, lunatic asylums would be empty. I came to that conclusion ages ago and long before reading Monday's *Daily Mail* in which some young people agreed to be interviewed and express their idiotic opinions on such trivia as life, love, sex, marriage and divorce. Normally I wouldn't dream of reading the opinions of pipsqueak teenagers but I was killing the longest half of the day, 10.30 – 11 a.m., and someone had left the *Mail* on the table in the patisserie I use as a waiting room. Anyway, what about Donna Wheeler, 18, catering assistant, Leicester? She said, 'First time I had sex, I was 16 and I hated it. It wasn't the way I imagined it would be. My mum told me that sex was wonderful if it was with the right person and I thought oh, this is going to be fantastic. Well, it wasn't and I felt disgusted with myself.' Quite so, and I must point out to teenage boys that this bears out an old adage of mine. Whenever you meet a pretty teenage girl always make a beeline for the mother. I've found it to be usually very rewarding.

On the touchy subject of abortion the *Mail* concludes that a third of the girls they spoke to disagree with the idea that abortion should be made legally available to all who want it. Looking at the teenagers around me I think it should be made compulsory. If ever I make anyone pregnant again – and I suppose I might in Pakistan, Wales on a Bank Holiday, or during the impending soda-water strike – I shall be only too well aware of the possible dangers. Just imagine having a baby son – called Darren on his mother's insistence – who'd grow up to read the *Sun*, get tattooed, ride a moterbike and drink light ale out of cans while watching breakfast television. Alternatively you might sire a daughter – called Trish by her mother – who'd grow up to work in an advertising agency, wear sunglasses on the top of her head, frequent discos and describe everything as being 'brilliant'. No, the human race has been battling long enough and should declare its innings closed.

On the very beautiful subject of marriage, Alexandra Duce, 19, classics student, Leeds University, says, 'Marriage is out-dated. I don't see the need to legalise a relationship with a scrap of paper.'

What a terrible thing to say. I suspect a printer's error here and that Ms Duce is at Leeds *United*. Marriage is the opium of the mentally unstable. A truly wonderful thing if a trifle addictive. And as for 'trial' marriages, they interviewed a really crafty one in Marc Chambers-Willis, 16, son of a former nurse, London. He said, 'I'd definitely want to live with the girl I wanted to marry first, so that if at the last moment we knew marriage would be wrong for us, we could back out.' What a cheek! My advice to young Marc Chambers-Willis is that if he wants to have the leg over and then *back out* as he calls it – and he clearly intends just that – then he should never give his right name, it being as memorable as his mother's present occupation. (I must change my occupation on my passport to 'former schoolboy'.)

We now come to divorce, not a pretty subject, and a 16-year-old schoolboy, Jason White, knows it all. 'I'm never going to get divorced. When I marry, I'm going to make sure the marriage works.' Well, well. What Master White should be pondering is the far more profound problem of how to make his divorce work. Speaking as a man who's been through three of the wretched redundancies I can tell you and him that it's not easy. Take my last wife. We get on like a house on fire. Last week she took me out to a splendid dinner, she buys me presents, calls me 'old bean' and even phones the Coach & Horses to see whether I've snuffed it or not. But final and damning proof of the failure of our divorce is that she *still* laughs at my jokes. I wouldn't swap her for a wife.

Away from it all

The literature on my bookshelves is gathering dust. There are only two things I read now, quite obsessionally too, and they are travel brochures and cookery books. Byron has been ousted by Elizabeth David, and the *Sporting Life* has been replaced by guides to the Greek Islands, Istanbul and India. Exactly three years ago I managed to get a free trip to Barbados and the following year I earned myself a holiday on the island of Serifos by writing some stultifying soft pornography which would have made a satyr yawn. But it was Barbados that spoilt me. Now, as Charlie addresses me on the price of satsumas in Berwick Street market, as Norman Balon unfolds his philosophy, and as Julia reiterates that she doesn't fancy me, all I can hear is the surf, the thud of a falling coconut, the comforting tread of an approaching waiter accompanied by the reassuring tinkle of ice against glass and, with luck, the soothing and distant screams of German and Swedish tourists drowning in the foaming undertow.

Norman brings me back to earth for a moment by throwing a menu at me. 'Are you going to eat?' he snarls. 'We've got steak pie, chicken and mushroom pie, savoury mince and toad in the hole. Hurry up. Someone wants your fucking table.' But I drift away again. Sitting beneath the palms, sheltered from the throb of the sun, I can hear the fizz of frying prawns, the dying hiss of a lobster and the rattle of a cocktail shaker and, with luck, the scream of a German tourist treading on a sea urchin. Norman, damn him, breaks the spell again. 'Here you are, large vodka, put your own fucking ice in and give me a pound.' Insensitive to his charm I drift off to Serifos to watch the fishing boats come back across that clear, sparkling blue. The waiter brings me another ouzo and in the back of the taverna the soft chunks of spicy lamb are nearly ready. Just as it's about to be served, someone shouts across the bar, 'Ere, Jeff. Broadsword won the first. Two to one.' I'm disgusted. If Doctor bloody Johnson had ever walked down a gangplank in Bridgetown and spent a morning catching his clap there, or if he'd ever had an afternoon nap in a citrus grove, then we wouldn't have had that daft utterance about London and not getting tired of it (a man, like him, who has an opinion on *everything* can be a bore).

But here we are in the grey, damp gloom of Greek Street, caught up in the exhausting career of doing absolutely nothing and hanging on by our fingertips in intensive care on a Smirnoff drip. But there are, of course, holidays I wouldn't swap for this weather and waste of life. Last Sunday, on Cliff Michelmore's holiday spot on television, we were treated to a run-down on Rimini and guided through it by a woman who'd holidayed there. The idea of sharing a beach with a bigger crowd than the one that gathers at Wembley on Cup Final day, living on pizza, plonk and pasta and whiling away the evenings in discos nearly made me throw up. It looked worse than the first holiday I ever had after leaving school.

That was in 1949. Two of us plus two girls rented a caravan of all things at Newhaven of all places. The caravan itself was infested with earwigs, in the evenings we were continually dive-bombed by maybugs, on an outing to Brighton one day I got hit over the head

A little bit drunk. Francis Bacon and me in the Colony Room Club in 1971.

by a billiard cue – the handle end is weighted, you know – in a sleazy billiard hall and, finally, the calor gas stove blew up in the face of my partner causing her a sudden lack of interest in the proximity of my perfectly formed body. Shock, I suppose. But in those days I used to find it almost impossible to be in the dumps on hot, sunshine-filled days. Even being skint was just about bearable. If you took up your sunbathing position on the pavement outside the French pub, sooner or later someone in funds would cool you down with a beer.

Further back, I remember school holidays being pretty ghastly. I spent every day dreading the return to school and the anxiety made me feel quite ill. Anyway, there was very little to do in Holland Park in the Forties apart from trying to destroy it. I was fond of throwing stones through people's windows, popping thunderflashes through their letter boxes and burning things down from my mum's summer house to half of an unkempt Ladbroke Gardens. They saved the resident barrage balloon. Thank God I've nearly grown up and now take my holidays a bit more seriously. Next month I hope to be writing to you from India. I can hardly wait for the diarrhoea and the vodka drought. Meanwhile, I wish Norman would leave me to my Caribbean and Mediterranean dreams.

Fresh start

Breakfast television is something of a boon to a man who wakes up, stares at the ceiling and wonders what the hell he did last night and what he's going to do today. To sit in bed with my first cup of steaming Earl Grey to find Anna Ford discussing female circumcision was a wonderful experience. I've done some incredible and strange things in my bed but I can't remember any of them having resulted in laughter before. Tears, yes (in the summer of 1979 I seriously considered buying a rubber sheet). Usually I wake up with Patricia Hughes, two eyes that feel like fried eggs and a mouth like an ash tray, but since Anna has graced my bedroom, I can't wait to wake up and the bags under my eyes seem to me to indicate that I'm giggling in my sleep. It's early stages yet but my one worry about Frosty and Anna's programme is that it's going to have a feminine bias. Why wasn't mine host Norman hauled into the studio to discuss male circumcision? Charity begins at home and I'm far more concerned about what goes on in Golders Green than the happenings in the Sudan.

What I'd very much like to see is a slot for men called 'Where were you last night?' They could bring in almost any man off the street and have him grilled by Irma Kurtz and then slapped on the wrist by Anna Raeburn. I'd also like to see my own slot in which I'd concoct a hangover drink and breakfast cure (kedgeree, a crème-de-menthe-based cocktail and a cheque in the post, for example), and a man could swap punches with the likes of the 'Peace' women who beat up Heseltine, and quite rightly too. There are quite a lot of men too – talking of peace – who aren't hell-bent on a nuclear holocaust, but they never get a look-in with the media. But it's nice to see a female gardener for a change and one with the obligatory Hampshire accent. The riddle is how they get Hazel Evans to the studio on time since she's never got to the Coach on time. And the same goes for Irma who has often soothed this agonised uncle over a jar.

Yes, I've my own gardener and aunt and all I need now is

someone to tell me whether or not it's raining outside. Much as I like the Commander I find him a trifle flamboyant and I'd like to see a no-nonsense Charlie do the weather spot occasionally. It would simply be, 'It's pissing down in Scotland and there'll be a force 7 skirtlifter from the West.' But although I said I was worried about the female bias I do think that women should be allowed a shot at the weather: 'It's a perfectly wonderful day and there's no need for you to be cooped up in the pub all day.' There's also room for a woman doctor who could demonstrate home vasectomies to housewives and a Closed University for truants.

But if we are to be faced by women on breakfast television can we please have some ordinary, middle-aged boilers? It's ridiculous that you have to be what the public in general consider to be glamorous to read the wretched news. Personally, Angela Rippon's eyes remind me of Tony Zale's eyes. He was middleweight champion of the world in 1946 and after, and if looks could kill – never mind the left hook. I'm not squeamish, not even at 8 a.m. and I'd even watch one of my ex-wives read the news, but I suppose we're lumbered with these well-packaged jobs for ever.

Breakfast apart, I accidentally caught the evening job documentary about how much harm alcohol does to people. Who on earth do they get to research such stuff? School leavers? What nonsense. Practically everybody I know should have been dead years ago. But alcohol and television go well together. At weekends particularly, now, television is so bad you have to be drunk to watch it, even if it does mean having to keep one eye closed to see just the one set. But I've hardly had a drink since this morning nonsense began. I get enough kicks from Anna and Dave to last me the day.

Jogging along

When the lease of this body I live in expires I hope to be buried in Canada. It was there, a few days ago, that a gravedigger was sacked for being too cheerful. Apparently he whistled and hummed while acting as a pall-bearer at a cemetery. Another time he held up a skull to his colleagues, while they were shifting remains from one grave to another, wearing a large grin on his face. I like it. I know I shall go to the grave kicking and screaming but there's no need for anybody else to join in the hysteria. Mind you, what these people actually whistle is quite important. I'd prefer to go out to 'Goodnight Ladies' than 'I Know That My Redeemer Liveth', because I know no such thing. Anyway, the vicar of Chaddleworth once told me that I was beyond redemption. A pretty shitty thing for a vicar to say, by the way, but he had been at the Bells. (Appropriately, the slogan on their labels is 'Afore Ye Go' and I'd like to suggest to the Smirnoff people that they adopt 'Just the One' as their slogan.)

Yes, what with all the recent digs, I've been more than usually preoccupied with death. The other night I had one of the worst attacks of angst I've ever suffered. I was utterly exhausted but I didn't dare close my eyes so convinced was I that if I did then I'd never wake up again. But, as you can see, I did, and to the good news of the jolly gravedigger. The bad news was an article about how to achieve longevity, jogging, health food, taking care of one's body and all the rest of that area of nonsense. I do wish people would stop telling me what I 'ought' to do. It's so bloody Germanic.

Anyway, we elected a new member to the low life hall of fame last week – the jazz man who died aged 100. Just before he snuffed it, on the actual birthday itself, he uttered the immortal words, 'If I'd known I was going to live this long I would have taken better care of myself.' Marvellous stuff. He'd smoked from the age of six and all his life he'd refused to drink water. Now that's what I call a marathon and it puts this smoker-since-14 and Perrier addict firmly in my place. Quite obviously our hero must have carefully avoided free-range corn flakes and any form of exercise for 100 years. As I've said before just what the hell do these health freaks want to get fit *for*? Cranks is a damned good name for a health food chain and, by God, don't the customers therein look absolutely ghastly? Joggers too, like militant feminists, tend to look pretty unattractive and a three-mile canter isn't going to turn a toad into a prince. I can suddenly visualise Cyril Connolly filling up with muesli, donning shorts and then running round the park, and it's ridiculous. I think jogging might be rather like listening to pop music on earphones all day in so far as both occupations relieve their mindless followers of the burden of actually having to *think*.

There are far less strenuous ways of avoiding constructive thought, such as reading the *Sun*, masturbating or listening to Norman Balon on the subject of the Middle East. Jogging, eating bran and most forms of abstinence are about a futile effort to avoid death. I remember Maurice Richardson once telling me, 'I don't read the obituaries any more. Death has lost its charm for me.' If only he'd lived to read about the Canadian gravedigger. Perhaps the reaper isn't so grim. I'd like to think that one day our man in Toronto – if he gets another job – will hold up my petrified pancreas to his mates, positively wreathed in smiles. I had intended to leave my body to the hepatic experts of the Royal Free Hospital, not to further science but to relieve Norman of the burden of a whip round in the Coach for the funeral expenses. But now it has to be a single to Canada, a perch in a cosy bar and then a wait. Life is a waiting room anyway. Sometimes I think I can hear the station announcer: 'Owing to an unforeseen fault – a strong constitution -- and a refusal to take the timetable seriously, death will not arrive until tomorrow.' And, as far as waiting rooms go, it's not too bad. There are plenty of cigarette machines, plenty of steaks, ice cream, chocolate cakes, booze and you don't *have* to eat the nut cutlets or jog up and down the platform. Yes, tomorrow will do.

Taxing

If there are as many as 1,760 readers of this wretched column with current accounts in the black I'd be obliged if they'd sponsor me to run a mile at the rate of £1 per yard. It would almost exactly pay the bill I've just received from the Inland Revenue; £176 would just about kill me but £1,760 is a joke and utterly beyond me. As an estimate on the part of these tax officials it proves that their heads are even more deeply submerged in the sand than mine. Never mind, I've still got three days before they take me to court or start distraint proceedings or both. Of course, running a mile would kill me but that too would cancel the bill. What I also need, and it may be too late, is an accountant and one who can grasp just how much it takes in the way of expenses to lead and write about the low life. It's cold outside and if you're not on the firm or on the staff then you're in the shit. Only workaholic writers like Benny Green survive, and they can work and write so much because, luckily for them, they have the extraordinary idea that what they churn out is good. If a man's pleased with himself he can make money.

Right, having got that whinge out of the way I shall proceed to break down my day in the hope that someone at the Inland Revenue will appreciate just how much it costs to do absolutely nothing without expenses. Morning tea, Kleenex, cigarettes, phone call to apologise for night before £2. Copy of the *Times* and hair of the dog £1.40. Taxi to the Coach & Horses (unable to walk, too down at heel) £1.60. Three large vodkas by myself to face oncoming day £3. Drinks for information, gossip, dirty jokes, tall stories and autobiographical reminiscences from Charlie, Conan, Jeremy and No Nickers Joyce £6. Two more large vodkas by myself to keep going £2. Chicken in lemon sauce, beef with spring onions and ginger, mixed vegetables in Jubilee Dragon to sooth infuriated pancreas £6.50. Iodine, sticking plaster and bandages for wounds inflicted by Chinese waiters £1.75. Drinks and fruit machine in afternoon club £6. Returned favourite 3.30 Kempton Park £5. Refresher course of vodkas in Coach at 5.30 £7. Taxi home £1.60. Money for old rope for suicide attempt £3.50. Long-distance phone calls to friends in middle of night to moan, whine and complain £4.75.

Now something out of that lot has to be tax deductible. But take a day out of Soho. In an hour's time I'm off to Bristol University to speak to the students. God knows why. I've got nothing to say, but it may sell a *Spectator* or two. Anyway, apart from the fare being £24 return, I shall need four large ones for Dutch courage and at BR prices that's about £7.20. Then, drinks for students and drinks for my wounded pride on the way home and you can see that it's pretty easy when you suffer from fiscal haemophilia. The thing is, if you work from 9 to 5 in an office, then you can't spend money.

Now, apart from tax, I'm being sued by a company for £500. More folly. For years and years alchemists the world over tried to make gold and they only turned to that daft pursuit after having spent 3,000 years trying to get blood out of stones. You'd think history would teach someone something. But no. If things get much worse I might have to buy a bugle and start practising the Last Post.

Oddly enough, I did have an idea about how to make some money the other day if only I could get it off the ground. I should have thought American tourists, for example, might be getting heartily sick of seeing the Tower of London and the Abbey etc. In conjunction with some hideous place like the Hilton why not, I thought, organise a low-life sightseeing tour of this stinking metropolis? At £100 each a day a coach load would gross £5,000. For that they could get thrown out of the Swiss Tavern, visit a betting

The sack from the *Sporting Life* in 1971. A slightly pompous letter.

shop, have a typically English meal thrown at them by Norman, meet a bailiff, get taken to Wormwood Scrubs by a tipstaff, and wake up the following morning skint on a park bench before going to court. If I can get this one going I reckon I could earn £30,000 a week. Very nearly as much as Benny Green and Frederick Forsyth put together.

Indisposed

At last, after years of trying, I've finally landed the Spring Double. Pneumonia *and* pleurisy. I wonder how much Ladbroke's would have laid me against getting the two? Anyway, I'm back in St Stephens Hospital where I was first shown the yellow card in December 1965. But this is the first time I've ever been in a hospital for something that wasn't self-inflicted and that makes it seem somehow a little unfair. They didn't *conscript* kamikaze pilots.

The ward I'm in is called Ellen Terry and down the corridor there's a ward called Alfred Tennyson. I tried to get moved to Benny Green or Larry Adler but they're completely filled with industrial accidents: people who've fallen into typewriters etc. There are six of us in Ellen Terry. Mr Rice opposite has a dodgy lung and he also has diarrhoea which he reports to me on in graphic detail every 30 minutes or so. I think I hate him. Next to him there lies a sheer hulk, poor Mr Collander, whose bladder is up the spout. Then there's Mr Handley, a costermonger from Fulham, who is rather delightful really and who has cancer of the lung. He quite rightly got a little crotchety with a young doctor last week who told him to give up smoking. As he said, 'A little late for that fucking advice, isn't it?' My chest man and registrar is all right though, even if he has developed the habit of draining my right lung via a needle inserted into it under my shoulder blade. Sadly, his students who play games with me preparatory to taking their finals all suffer from halitosis. A couple of them couldn't diagnose a decapitation but I gather they'll qualify.

What has been fascinating though, here in the bowels of Ellen Terry for the past three weeks, is the behaviour of the 'domestics'. Nearly all these ladies are West Indian, and by Christ what a mistake people make in thinking black is black and all the same. Africans are far more benign as a rule. But my *bête noire* is Granadian and we fell out a fortnight ago when I asked her to include a paper cup in the rubbish she was clearing away from the top of my locker. She erupted more rawly than the psoriasis in the next bed. 'I clean away shit,' she told me, 'and I clean away wine. I clear up tissues and wash glasses, but I don't touch paper cups.' Then, grabbing a handful of her own flesh, she went on, 'And this skin is black. Pure black. It's black, West Indian skin and what's more I know who my father is and I know who my mother is.' Never have I known such sudden paranoia. That evening Miss Barbados declared war too. She gave me a bowl of soup but wouldn't give me a spoon. 'I serve soup,' she said, 'but I never have anything to do with spoons.' 'Particularly white men's spoons,' she muttered under her breath.

But open warfare has existed since I became addicted to tea twenty days ago. Not a drink or a cigarette for twenty days and something had to give. (Are addicts addicted to addiction?) I must have continuous tea now. I chain-drink the stuff but I'm not allowed in the kitchen to boil the water for my tea bags and the West Indians watch me like hawks. I run dangerous gauntlets to boil water. Yes, it's quite a serious place is the Ellen Terry Ward and you don't have to behave that eccentrically to get into their bad books or get classified as I have by Sister as being a 'difficult patient'. Only the other night as they were doing their final round with the drugs trolley I asked the staff nurse in charge of the amazing vehicle, 'Do you have anything to make love last?' *Eine kleine Nacht* aside, but that nurse has been off me ever since. This is a very serious place and if my friend Mr Handley doesn't start taking his impending death a little more seriously he could be in for some cold treatment. Meanwhile, the cockles of my heart have been wonderfully warmed by the amazingly kind and touching get well cards and letters I've received from readers of this column since I've been in Ellen Terry. What a nice lot you sound. And now for two weeks' convalescence. My man with the long needles has told me to do absolutely nothing when I get home. That shouldn't be too difficult.

Big guns

In the past, I've always resolved to while away those endless hours of boredom while held prisoner in a hospital bed by reading those books I've never got around to but which I've stupidly felt *obliged* to read. *The Mill on the Floss* and yet another attempt at *Ulysses*, for example. But it doesn't work. Reading can be hard work and too much for a sick man. You have to be pretty fit to read Bernard Levin on Soviet dissidents, but to get through *The Mill on the Floss*, Proust or even the more recent and slender but overrated *French Lieutenant's Woman* while stuffed with more tubes than the London Underground system, you need to be a marathon man capable of beating Jack Dempsey after 26 miles. What I did get stuck into though was a load of hospital C.S. Forresters. The 'Hornblower' books. I liked them when I first read them and they stand up well. Excellent, lightish, stirring stuff. Anyway, I've always been a fan of Nelson and his colleagues and recent events in Europe have in no way diminished my wish to blow a few Frenchmen and their ships clean out of the water.

But there I was in St Stephens, no 74-gun ship of the line, but a mere sloop shipping water, short of provisions and out of powder. Ever since I've been back here in port licking my wounds I keep looking at the captain's log book for that last day of memorable action in St Stephens. Cape St Vincent palls beside it. Anyway, three days ago, I awoke at 3 a.m. and lay there tossing in my hammock until 6 a.m. I was desperate for my fix of tea and by 6.15 a.m. when the West Indian enemy still hadn't hove in sight with the tea trolley, I made my own way with my tea bag and limped to the kitchen. All seemed quiet and deserted. I put the tea bag in the cup, boiled the kettle and then, too late, I heard it – the rustle of a dress. It could have been the crack of a mainsail. My inbuilt lookouts, utterly exhausted, were asleep. I turned round and, clapping my reading glasses to my good eye, I beheld the awesome sight of Fernanda, the gorgon of Granada, bearing down on me, her top gallants straining in front of the wind. There was no time to bequeath my dear Susan to the nation or to run up a patriotic signal. This mere sloop, as redundant as a dinghy at Trafalgar, was suddenly about to be engaged by the 136-gun, Santissima Trinidad, the biggest warship afloat. Vainly I swung the wheel hard to port but her first shot knocked the cup out of my hand and sent boiling water everywhere. 'You not supposed to be here,' she screamed. 'Dis my kitchen. Get de fuck out.' Now she was wrestling the kettle away from my grasp and, weak, panting and undermanned as it were, the last thing I could afford was a Rastafarian boarding party. I backed away and dropped anchor by the fridge. She stood by the sink riding the swell, a master gunner wearing gold-rimmed bi-focals and peering down the barrel to judge another broadside.

There are, thank God, and always have been, moments of inspiration that have changed the course of history and as my right

96

Jacki Ellis, my second wife, who was acting at the Old Vic when I was a stage hand there. Photographed by John Deakin, 1960.

hand suddenly felt the comforting lump of a half pound of butter I knew she was but a Rupert to my Cromwell. I had offered my kingdom for a horse and got Shergar. The butter hit her on the left shoulder with such force she spun round and dropped the kettle. Making full sail and all speed she sailed past me, screaming, to take refuge in Alfred Tennyson ward. I could hear her in the distance as I refilled the kettle. 'De man in Ellen Terry, Mister Bernard, he fucking mad. Try to kill me. He cut my arm wid butter. Crazy man.' It was a momentous victory. Britannia rules the kitchen.

Of course, there were diplomatic peace talks as I lay in the cockpit panting, trembling and almost vomiting after the strain, the loss of temper and what you might call the exercise. A friendly Jamaican envoy, the night sister from Alfred Tennyson, brought me more tea and soothed my fevered brow as the church bells rang out the length and breadth of England. At midday I came home. Whether I can take two more weeks in bed, even at home, I'm not sure. I still can't read a major opus and when I dipped into Carola Oman's *Nelson* last night it made me restless and I lay here fretfully, longing for action again and my own 74-gun command in a really big hospital like the Bellevue in New York. I'd give them a tea-bag party that would make the Boston one look sick. But it's all brought one thing home. My body wants no more of the low life. It's in a dreadful state and it wants mollycoddling.

By the way, there have been more lovely cards and notes from readers, whom I thank from the bottom of my pacemaker. To them I shall reveal in my will where I've hidden the tea bags.

Saturday fever

It seems to me that the League Against Cruel Sports only opens its mouth to change step. One expects a load of horse manure during Grand National week but if these people were really concerned about cruel sports you'd think they'd be venting their concern on such cruelties as getting married, having a family, eating in Trust House Forte establishments, the licensing laws and editors who can do without me. One horse, Duncreggan, did get killed, having received the kiss of death the day before when I drew him in the *Spectator* sweep, but if he'd got killed at Southwell or Plumpton on a Monday afternoon you wouldn't have heard a dicky bird.

And oddly enough, talking of getting killed, I nearly died laughing on the morning of the National when I read in the 'Notebook' (9 April) that our old friend Geoffrey Wheatcroft spends his Saturday mornings doing a little work in the Reading Room of the British Museum when he's stuck in London. Pull the other one. I know for a fact that when he says he's off to a recital in Smith Square he is in fact off to the Savile Club to play snooker. But don't think I'm getting at Geoffrey. I remember well just how important this sort of thing was before I had my own library, record collection and games room. Mind you, I was lucky enough to have been steeped in culture and scholarship from the word go, so it's all water off a duck's back to me and hardly worth mentioning; suffice it to say that my mother left me in a Fortnum's carrier bag on the steps of the London Library when I was an hour old. That was a Saturday morning in 1932 and I believe my mother had been browsing in Hatchards when she gave birth to me in the poetry department. At the same time, my father was preparing for the event just up the road, browsing in Cogswell & Harrison for a pair of 12-bores.

Yes, Saturday mornings have become one hell of a problem. Geoffrey went on to say that after the literary grind he goes on to shop in Soho and then to do some drinking in El Vino. Luckily for me I was brought up by my foster parents – my foster father was the chief librarian of the Bodleian – to make my own pasta, so I've never had to join that precious throng of BBC Talks Producers who walk up and down Old Compton Street on Saturday mornings clutching sprigs of fennel and would-be bedside lamps in the shape of chianti bottles. Not that you see much of that sort of thing nowadays. What's screwed up Saturday in London, deadened it if you like, is that nearly everyone now has a weekend cottage, or invitation to one. If you haven't been invited to an 'in' county for the weekend by a Tarquin, Rupert, Cassandra or Candida you can count yourself dead or dead drunk in El Vino. This is, of course, a large helping of sour grape juice on my part. There's nothing I like more on a Saturday morning than sitting on Jasper and Letitia's sofa sipping a stingy bloody mary, scratching myself and my last two 10p pieces together and listening to them saying that things have got so bad they can barely pay the gardener, the bill for the logs, Eton and the second Range Rover, and that they're very much afraid that lunch is lamb and not beef.

But to go back to the League Against Cruel Sports for a moment, it's on these weekend occasions that they're conspicuous by their absence. Letitia and Jasper always have six children – they're either practising Catholics or they conceive in post-Badminton Horse Trial euphoria – called Sebastian, Benjie, Magnus, Samantha, Arabella and Sabrina. At weekends, starting on Saturday morning when Geoffrey is pretending to read Pascal in the original but in fact making out a Soho shopping list, these children completely take over the house. Darling Bashy knocks your vodka out of your hand, Benjie stands on your balls, and Magnus sticks his finger in your eye. Letitia, vaguely spotting all this, stirs herself and says, 'Oh *do* come along darlings, I'm sure Jeff doesn't want you doing that.' These children should of course be put down like Duncreggan or put out to grass until they're 21. They throw jam at you at tea time, cheat at Monopoly, cry when they lose, have epileptic fits at bed time and they know at a glance that the clothes you stand up in are the only ones you've got or very nearly.

On reflection, Geoffrey Wheatcroft has it right. Saturday mornings can be well obliterated in the British Museum and, as he admits, there's no need to tarry after opening time when Pascal gives way to Man on the Spot, Augur and The Scout. But I have, and always have had, my doubts about a Saturday drink in El Vino. Imbibing with hacks and solicitors is another thing the League Against Cruel Sports should look into. Meanwhile it's back to bed for me for another week where Saturday is much like any other day.

Comeback

The comeback trail, as that unprepossessing would-be, Joe Bugner, could testify, is one hell of a slog, pitted with potholes and boredom. I thought I'd retired and that the days of tight-rope walking and hustling were over. There I was, lying on my bed, sipping tea and watching the Embassy World Snooker Championship on television when my manager phoned up out of the blue. His old, familiar and horrible voice had my adrenalin pumping in seconds. 'What's the matter, have you given up or something?' 'No, Norman,' I said. 'In fact I'm feeling much better.' 'Well then, if you're not bleedin' dying why don't you look into the Coach? I mean, don't fucking give up, eh?' It was like hearing the bells for 'seconds out' again.

I dropped my insulin into the wastepaper basket, opened a packet of digestive biscuits – the ones with plain chocolate on one side – and stared at the old-fashioned tumbler full of swizzle sticks that was gathering dust with other souvenirs like my typewriter on the desk. I got up and looked at myself closely in the mirror. Was I too old to drink again? Had the head, legs and pockets gone? Norman had said, 'You can always drink Perrier, you know', before he'd rung off, but the sound of his voice had me suddenly longing for those 10-and-12-round bouts again. To hell with starting at the bottom again. The lure of the main event was as strong as ever. There I was, sitting on my stool in the corner. Norman bent over me flapping a tea-cloth in my face and pressing a £20 note to my jacket pocket and whispering urgently, 'You'll need twenty more stitches there later but you've got him now.' I eyed my opponent, a particularly successful friend, but he looked depressingly strong. True, I'd outfumbled him for eight rounds, but he was still there. Norman pushed me off my stool and out again and for one second, a split second, I dropped my guard and smiled. I never even heard the bell for last orders. I heard my voice feebly asking, 'Where am I?' and someone answered, 'It's all right champ, you're in the Colony Room Club.' You win some, you lose some.

I shook myself out of the daydream and took another close look at the old face. My eyes were quite white for the first time in eight weeks and the tell tale angry red denoting liver damage had vanished from the palms of my hands. I was ready to spar if not fight. I got my kit out of the wardrobe – the old jeans and jersey that brought me luck – put them on and then stepped out into the roar of Great Portland Street. I bobbed and weaved my way down to Piccadilly avoiding the Stags Head, George and Woodcock – something told me I wasn't quite ready – and walked into the tea room of Fortnums.

Within 15 minutes, after a pot of tea and a scone, I realised I'd walked into a hornet's nest. Those crazy sessions in the Coach and all over Soho palled beside Fortnums. This was where the champions hung out. The hardest bunch of nuts I've ever found myself in the midst of. At the next table there sat six Iranian students sipping lemon tea and counting travellers' cheques. In a far corner the ex-film star, Terence Stamp, sat pretending to learn some lines and at the next table a varnished, lacquered, dyed blond sat yawning

101

opposite her 70-year-old meal, clothes, rent and holiday ticket. I was joined by an American tourist who ordered a peach melba and who then said, 'Sure is one hell of a place, your London.'

I threw in the towel and the waitress took nearly ten minutes to bring me the bill. For the same money I could have had a harmless vodka in the cosy comfort of the Coach with the added bonus of Norman propelling me from my corner at the sight of a new punter like a man saying 'bone' to a dog. Make no mistake, the Fortnums mob are like tempered steel. There's no Charlie there to press your head against the cool porcelain of the lavatory pan when you've been beaten. No Conan to tell you how to dodge the Tipstaff or Tom to tell you how to open a buff envelope. And I thought it was tough at the bottom. And what of the manageress of Fortnums? A Grenadier compared to Norman's Catering Corps NCO.

The comeback proper started in earnest yesterday. I had a glass of cider before lunch and went to my local instead of the corner shop for cigarettes, to drench myself in the atmosphere again. It stinks but it's the stink I know.

Finders keepers

There's something slightly obscene about the American obsession with litigation, but then, with a handful of exceptions like Lincoln, W.C. Fields, Flash Gordon and Rocky Graziano, they always have had their values all wrong. The latest nutcase is a 30-year-old unemployed docker called Joey Coyle I read about in Tuesday's *Standard*. He found $1.2 million (about £756,000) in the street in Los Angeles and is suing the owner of the money because he says it has ruined his life by giving him a taste of how the other half lives. Mr Coyle went on a little spending spree, and when the police found him two weeks later when he was down to his last $105,000, a paltry £64,000, which he had stuffed in his boots. To cap it all an insane jury accepted his plea of temporary insanity and found him not guilty. I'd very much like to know just how he knocked out the odd £692,000 in two weeks and I'd very much like to have a lawyer with the gall to stand up in court and say, 'My client has suffered severe psychological disruption and mental instability. If the security

Jill, my third wife and mother of my daughter Isabel.

company (who lost the money) had been more careful my client would not have been damaged.'

Speaking as a middle-man I have had mouth-watering tastes and sick-making tastes of how both other halves live and I can't say that either have ruined my life; such a hefty sum is a punch that a one-time docker should be able to ride in comfort. A man who'd spent his entire life living at one extreme or another I could feel sorry for, but Mr Coyle, at some time pretty comfortably employed if our lads in Wapping and Liverpool have been anything to go by, should be able to regard a million-dollar windfall as a mere loan from the Almighty and proof that every time it rains it rains dollars from heaven. It's nothing to go mad over.

But take the very disturbing opposite end of the fiscal spectrum and consider just how awful and brain-damaging it could be for the Duke of Westminster or Lord Howard de Walden to find a fiver in the street. 'Duke found wandering in Grosvenor Street, mumbling incoherently and talking gibberish. Police say the Duke went missing yesterday and was found with 5p in his shoe. In a statement last night the Duchess said, "Buffy must have been absolutely shattered to find such a small sum. We're trying to retrace his footsteps and we'd very much like to contact the man who saw him buy a half of bitter and a cheese roll in the Antelope." Inspector Smith of the Chelsea police who is leading the investigation said that they are working on the theory that the fiver was dropped by a dropout. A tramp is believed to be helping them with their inquiries. The Westminster family motto is "Spend, spend, spend".'

One can only hope that Mr Coyle gave most of the £692,000 away as well as buying himself a headache and AIDS. But forgetting him for a moment, if you need further proof that Americans are mad – all right, naïve – then what about a ridiculous book just published by two of their doctors called *How to Control Your Drinking*. This is claimed to be a self-help book which shows that an alcoholic doesn't have to abstain for ever. In my opinion the barman in *Lost Weekend* had it right when he told Ray Milland, 'One's too many and a hundred's not enough.' But Messrs Miller and Munoz don't agree, and in this ridiculous book they list alternatives to getting drunk when getting drunk is what you want. They advocate relaxation when the thirst hits you and they recommend 'Waiting in line (American for queueing). Riding a bus. Doing housework. Playing ping-pong. Talking to a very angry person. Taking care of an emergency.'

Playing ping-pong? I ask you. As for an emergency, could there be a bigger one than queueing up in the Coach with a glass of Perrier in one hand waiting to play ping-pong with Norman just as he's been told by his mother that she's leaving all her money to me? Could this really help keep one moderately sober? But relaxation isn't enough. According to Miller and Munoz you have to be assertive as well as relaxed to drink moderately and control it. And they give the readers a list of assertive remarks to trot out when you're screaming for the Smirnoff. 'I don't like being called honey.' 'I really enjoyed that dessert.' 'I am very angry with you.' Only if I'd met Mr Coyle when he found his million dollars, and he'd taken me out to dinner and then refused to lend me any money could I justifiably say anything like that.

Dear Diary

I was deeply disappointed that Hitler's diaries turned out to be fakes but I wasn't in the least surprised. He was far too unstable, I thought, to keep a diary and anyway the madness and evil of his day-to-day existence was always going to ensure that he wouldn't be forgotten. He's always held a morbid fascination for me and even now, when I see a photograph of him, I feel a sort of unbelieving and bewildered horror such as I experience when I'm drinking coffee in Maison Valerie and find muself surrounded by women dressed from jumble sales and reading the *Guardian*. But anyway, when I told you the other day that I'd been sorting out old papers, letters and snapshots, I forgot to tell you that I found two diaries: one for 1975 and the other for 1978. Sadly, the *Sunday Times* are unlikely to offer me a single, lousy penny for them – they like to keep their diaries benign and bland – but I do think I ought to now own up to a few entries before they're unearthed in thirty years' time in the cellar of the Coach & Horses and have doubts cast on their authenticity. As I said, Hitler was far too unstable to keep a diary; to address such a book, day in and day out, the author needs both feet firmly on the ground plus the sincere intention of plodding towards the grave with a sober, realistic tread devoid of fantasy, anger, paranoia and self-pity, simply recording the beauty and wonder of the daily round.

With that in mind I find it rather strange that my entry for Friday 4 April 1975 should read: 'I find it almost impossible to believe that anyone can be as unhappy as I am. Can misery cause insanity? Saved by a 32-1 double at Sandown Park.' Happily, I must have come back down to earth a week later, when I see I wrote: 'Met a very nice girl called Valerie at a party in Hampshire. She asked me what sign I was and when I said Gemini she said, "So was my father. I killed him in a car crash and when they took him to hospital they found a dozen french letters in his pocket." I cheered her up by telling her that he must have had a lot of love to give around. Driven back to London with John Le Mesurier by a man whose hobby is flying a Spitfire.'

Well, whoever it was who said – and I think it was me – life is ghastly and boring and the good days are the exception and not the rule, got it right. I doubt very much whether Hitler ever spent his birthday, 20 April, like: 'Went to launderette and sat there wondering where on earth Miss Right is.' On the other hand you wouldn't be bowled over with surprise if he'd written as I did for 22 April: 'Had tea with Caroline who told me that she's "very serious" about a major in the Household Cavalry.' But when you can't get any lower you have to surface, and by 1978, three years later to the week, the launderette had closed, Caroline had vanished into Knightsbridge Barracks and Barbara had appeared. 'Barbara came over for lunch and then we had a row in bed. She kept on talking about her shopping expeditions while I was feeling terrible about being skint. Eventually it was all right and she drove me to the Chelsea Arts Club. In a very tense foursome, partnered by a dentist, I potted the last four colours to win a good game. After, in the ladies bar, talked about insanity to Bill Redgrave and Freddie Deane.'

There must have been many days even in Hitler's life when he wouldn't have bothered to record, 'Eva came over for yoghurt tea and then drove me to the Chelsea Arts Club where, partnered by a dentist, I shot four people.' Yes, life is dull but there are odd, underlying mysteries in the most pedestrian of diary jottings. More from mine. 'Went to *Sunday Times* and spoke incoherently to Magnus Linklater about trip to Chantilly. Tea with Barbara who gave me book of love poems. Then delivered piece on Les Blair to Bob Smythe at the *Radio Times*. He mentioned Joan of Arc and I said she was such a bitch, if she was alive now she'd be a sub on the *Radio Times*.' A very silly day, by the sound of it, and matched only by a never-to-be-published entry made by Hitler: 'Went to Nuremberg and spoke incoherently to Keitel about trip to Moscow. Tea with Eva

106

With my daughter Isabel in 1975.

who gave me Shirley Conran's book on gardening. Delivered *Mein Kampf* to Frank Giles at the *Sunday Times*. Got advance on expenses. He mentioned Chamberlain who is, I believe, a sub on the *Sun*.'

Lucky Devils

My comeback was unintentional and it's been a little disappointing so far. You could say it was forced on me. I called into my ex-wife's office to have the weekly cup of tea with her. She was out but back in ten minutes, so I thought I'd kill the time by having just 'the one' in a revolting pub next door in Berwick market called the Blue Posts. Who should walk in but Norman Balon. I felt I'd been caught *in flagrante*. Not since Mavis's husband came home unexpectedly twenty years ago and found me sitting next to her, stark naked on a chaise-longue, have I felt such an utter shit. Out of bed at last and in the Blue Posts and not the Coach & Horses. Norman, of course, was doing his daily Soho round being bloody inquisitive and trying to assess how much more or less other pubs in the area were taking. So I had to go back to him and, unlike a lot of wives, he took me. Half an hour later I was in the Coach and having 'the one' as though I'd never left it.

One of the things I loathed most about school, the army and regular employment was the feeling that I was missing something and that in the pubs, clubs, cafés, dives and racecourse bars there was some sort of magic in progress that I wasn't able to conjure with. How must a bank clerk feel when he sees the clock moving towards opening time or the first race? So there I was in the Coach, back in the fold, and seeing for myself what I'd been missing. I must say Norman was charming. Some poor bastard, an absolute stranger who'd walked in for a quiet, small beer, was told: 'Get off that fucking stool and give it to Jeff here. He's sick.' No, nothing had changed. It was Friday and fish was on the menu and a few people were 'unwinding' after a hard week's slog in the office making personal telephone calls, stealing stationery and working out their expenses. A couple of pornographers were moaning about excessive police raids, someone said it hadn't been the same without me (better?), another person shook me by the hand, and many others said how well I was looking, although I know just how I look.

What did surprise me was everyone's astonishment that I was shortly off to Spain *alone*. Alone has very nearly become a dirty word. It's taken me about forty-nine years to get to not minding being alone, but it doesn't do to mention the fact publicly. Out of sheer, dreadful sentiment my heart used to bleed at such sights as a man or woman eating alone in a restaurant – on a Sunday particularly – but I think people are disturbed by someone being alone because they presume that he or she is automatically on the verge of suicide, living in squalor surrounded by dirty shirts and unwashed dishes and as friendless as a Getty. I've also been told that a man who lives alone forgets his manners since he's not always jumping up to open doors for ladies etc, but such a man should have at least one set of spare keys.

Anyway, if one person asked me, 'Haven't you got a girl you can take to Spain with you?', fifty did. Except for Norman, of course, who said I'd save money. No, I've had my share of holidays for two, and rubbing Ambre Solaire into someone's back while they read Harold Robbins and then suggest going somewhere miles away from a bar for a 'nice walk' isn't my idea of a healing fortnight. It's also a very dodgy business having a row with someone on holiday. You can't actually hide when you're sulking, and anyway you can only sulk until the next lousy meal brings you together again. A certain amount of sexual athleticism is also expected on holiday even when it's 95 in the shade and the cheap brandy is bubbling around in your gut. Then there's that dreadful foursome. Madame takes her head out of her paperback, spots another couple and in no time at all you're together having a drink as though it's Christmas. They tell you they come from Sidcup, Spokane or Perth and that last year they went to Majorca but they're not going to go back there ever again and that they're in a marvellous hotel that's only £10 a day. Then you pair off. He tells you that he's in computers and when you tell him you're a hack he says he can't say he's ever heard of you but you must meet some 'jolly interesting people'. Back at the hotel, between bouts of diarrhoea, Madam is not talking but pretending to read. Her shoulders are peeling and suddenly it's don't touch me time. A cockroach crawls out of your sponge bag and it occurs to you that by London time the Coach has just opened. You can almost hear them saying, 'Gosh, I bet they're having a marvellous time. Lucky devils.' What you do hear is, 'I hope you're not going to get drunk and be rude to that nice couple again.' Not for the next fortnight though.

Well mauled

William Harrison 'Jack' Dempsey, the 'Manassa Mauler' has taken the final count as *Ring Magazine* would, and will say. He was born on 24 June 1895 and was exceptionally well bred for the business of fighting, his ancestry being Irish-Scottish-Cherokee. He weighed 187lbs and he was 6ft 3/4in tall. Before Muhammad Ali, who tipped the scales at anything between 186lbs and 230lbs, all the class heavyweights were Dempsey's size and with the exception of the exceptional Ali they must have thrown three punches to the likes of Larry Holmes's one. But one from the likes of Dempsey or Louis could suffice. Some nut of a scientist in New York once fixed a mechanical device in the heavy bag at Stillman's Gymnasium and came up with the thought-provoking fact that a left hook from Joe Louis was the equivalent of a 90lb weight being dropped on your head from a height of 6ft. Not many hung around long enough to dispute the possibility, and Dempsey certainly hit as hard. Dempsey had, for the benefit of record freaks, a total of 80 fights of which he won 49 by the short route and he lost 7. Two of them of course, to Gene Tunney. And there's the crunch for me. Dempsey's death has me thinking of Tunney yet again and that's not to detract from the old mauler.

Years ago, there was an amusement arcade in the Charing Cross Road where for a couple of pence you could – and I did hundreds of times – see an old hand-wound flicker movie of Tunney beating Dempsey. I'm not here to revive memories of the famous 'long count' or to speculate as to whether Tunney could have survived after nine seconds but I do remember very well how extraordinarily vunerable Dempsey was to Tunney's overhand right crosses. That's why, I suppose, I have never been able to rate Dempsey in the top four. Comparisons may be odious but they kill the time of day. Tunney beat him decisively twice. Ali would have boxed his head off. Louis would have stopped him and Marciano was unstoppable. For all of that Dempsey was a great fighter who had a sort of uneducated ferocity that brought a glamour to the ring that died when Ali packed it in. In February 1926, Dempsey boxed twelve exhibition bouts in the space of one week, winning them all and eight of them by knockouts.

Even the names of his opponents have a ring about them that provokes the deepest nostalgia. Where are they now? Fireman Jim Flynn, Ed 'Gunboat' Smith, One-Round Garrison, Battling Levinsky and the Boston Bearcat. It makes you want to weep to look at Joe Bugner. Watching Dempsey chase Jess Willard around the ring when he won the world title is a remarkable reminder that the brother of the 'noble art' is that exciting animal the fighter. Pitted against each other Dempsey and Tunney were a pretty uncivilised spectacle that I find irresistible. Tunney psyched him, though, as well as outpointing him. Before the first fight the referee told Tunney, 'I don't want any squawks from the loser when this fight is over.' Tunney answered, 'Go over and tell that to Dempsey. He'll be more interested in what the loser has to say than I.'

But one of the more endearing human qualities is bravery. Guts come in all shapes and sizes. The little Lord Nelson had a hundred

With Susan Ashley, my fourth, last and most angry wife.

miles of them as did Edith Cavell, and Jack Dempsey wasn't the hero of thousands of young men in their day because of his patent leather shoes or flashing smile. (You have to be very well loved to smile like Errol Flynn or Dempsey.) There's something about boxers, though. I'm biased, having had a shot at it, but I soon realised in my Jack Solomon's Gymnasium days that they're the 'nicest' of sportsmen. When and if you can box and fight like 'Sugar' Ray Robinson you don't actually find it quite as necessary to be *nasty* to people. Temperament is part and parcel of it all, and John McEnroe, for example, will always be an arsehole as far as I'm concerned. No, it's all frightfully proper and upstanding even when the adrenalin is gushing. I like a piffling but touching quote from Tunney's autobiography, *A Man Must Fight*, concerning his last encounter. 'Jack greeted me as I entered the Ring: "How are you Gene?" "Quite well, Jack, and you?" I replied.'

Let mayhem commence. I seem to have been waffling more about

111

Tunney than Dempsey and what I meant to say was that Dempsey was a great fighter and one of the great sportsmen of this century. In the ghastly event of their being such a thing as a repeat known as an after life I imagine the aforementioned quote being reversed. 'Gene greeted me as I entered heaven. "How are you Jack?" "Quite well, Gene, and you?" ' He was *all* very well.

Train in Spain

It's widely claimed that it was W.C. Fields who uttered the immortal words 'Never give a sucker an even break', but it isn't so. God murmured them during an afternoon nap on the seventh day. A few million years later the Arabs coined the proverb, 'One minute, life is in your hand. The next minute, it's up your arse.' And three weeks ago I was kept awake all night by two nightingales who were singing in an orange tree outside the bedroom window of my Spanish villa. Well, it's not *my* villa actually, but you'd think a man could remove the nightingales before he lent you a few nights in the gardens of Spain. Keats, Granados, de Falla? Don't make me laugh.

But to start at the beginning, they said, 'Don't fly all the way. See Spain. Get the train from Madrid and see the countryside.' What they didn't say was, 'If you go by train the journey will take 13 hours and you'll be surrounded by Moroccan shepherds shitting on the floor.' Now I know that last bit may sound a little like a drunk with denture problems trying to sing a carol, but it's quite true. They're really amazing, are these people. Take me to the Race Relations Board if you like, but I'm here to tell you that the Arabs are quite ghastly. I don't mind them shoplifting in Marks and Spencer with £5,000 in their pockets – money *should* be reserved for self-indulgences – and I don't mind them squatting on the pavement outside my front door munching melons, but, when they've watched their flocks and then sold them I wish they'd go home by car. Anyway, I'd taken my right lung to Spain for an airing and that journey took another year off its life.

But I recovered over the next two days and, by a private pool in the sun that overlooked cork tree forests that went down to the shimmering sea, I gazed at the blue mountains of Africa beyond, full, no doubt, of shepherds shitting by their flocks. It was a heavenly sight; but God, omnipresent and not wanting to be outdone by his own work, had put a couple of vultures overhead in that heaven purely for my benefit. If it's not nightingales then it's vultures. Why I'd been picked on like this was my main preoccupation for the next few days as I loafed among the bars of Tarifa. It also occurred to me that if Norman put morsels of octopus, chorizo and salads on the bar in the Coach & Horses and if he also sold quadruple vodkas for 45p to the accompaniment of strumming guitars and clacking castanets then he wouldn't be a half bad bloke.

It was by the pool – put there by Him because I can't swim – one afternoon that I met Helen, the resident English widowperson. A delightful and friendly lady, she had merely two faults that I could see and hear: she said 'Well, this is it' in reply to everything I said, and she was accompanied everywhere by a dog called Roy. As Alan Rawsthorne once told me, 'Never trust a dog with an unsuitable name.' How right he was. Roy was right up Keats', Grandados's and de Falla's streets and he took up barking when the nightingales came off the night shift. But she was potty about dogs was Helen and there was a stray one nearby that she fed every day. She'd park her car precariously on the mountain road every morning, get out and whistle and then feed left-over french bread rolls to this thing that would come wagging out of the rocks. I mean, you just don't feed french bread to a dog. You might as well offer a cat a sandwich. Anyway, that was the routine every morning and after that she'd drive us to the market in Tarifa, or along the coast to a hotel owned by Nazi war criminals, where I'd have cocktails while she took Roy to the beach to bark at the bare breasts of tourists. I don't think anyone liked Roy very much.

So there I was getting a healthy tan in the middle of a scenic, culinary and alcoholic idyll when He Who Must Be Loved played his last card of the holiday. I was sitting by the pool one afternoon wondering if any of the local oranges would end up on Charlie's stall in Berwick Street when I suddenly got this God-awful pain in my chest. I guessed it might cost about £500 a week to be ill in Spain and anyway I want to be scattered in England and not fed to vultures or Roy. The only way I could get back to London was via Malaga and the only way I could get to Malaga was by taxi. Would you believe 160 kilometres in a taxi? It made my wallet break out in a sweat. Then the additional air fare to Madrid on top of that. Still, better than Moroccan shepherd smells. When I did get back I felt better. All a bit of a cockup, but that's life, or, as Helen would say, this is it.

Drip feed

I wasn't feeling very well last week. My man who dealt with my chest complaint impied that I might have lung cancer and the thought didn't concentrate the mind, as Doctor Johnson said, but dulled it and made the approach to this wretched typewriter something of an obstacle course. But last Monday, during a visit to Brampton Chest Hospital, a specialist told me that I had nothing 'sinister'. I drew a great breath of relief which made me cough for five minutes. Now this specialist struck me as being something of a shrewd nut. He guessed that I had the odd cigarette and cocktail, and how can you tell that looking at a bronzed Greek god across a desk in a consulting room, God only knows. What did fascinate me was the sight of my heart on the X-ray screen. It's there all right and it looks a lot bigger than it feels. Furthermore, it is not broken as I'd thought it was in an emotional accident I had in 1972 when Juliet told me for the last time, 'You make me sick.'

But what a bloody miracle this body is. If you fed into a cow or a horse what some of us consume in one day, what on earth would happen? I'd very much like to wake up one morning with a cow of the Friesian variety and walk her down to Soho to the Coach & Horses, stopping on the way to buy twenty Players, ply her with vodkas until closing time, whip her off to an Indian restaurant, take her up to the Colony Room Club till 5.30 and then to the Yorkminster, Swiss Tavern, Three Greyhounds, get beaten up by Chinese waiters at midnight, have a row with a taxi driver, set the bed on fire, put it out with tears and then wake up on the floor. Could you then milk the said cow? I doubt it.

During one of my animal visits to the great Fred Winter's yard I said to him, 'Good God, Fred, your horses look magnificent. Beautifully fit.' 'Of course they do, you twit,' he said. 'They don't sit up all night drinking gin and tonic and playing cards.' Anyway, although the past four months have been a bore and then a fright for me, I shall never be converted to jogging, wheat germ, deep-breathing exercises, free-range women or press-ups. It's put-downs and not press-ups that keep a man on his toes. But, as I say, this body never ceases to amaze me. It's very rebellious. It won't lie down. Now that the right lung is mere scar tissue it comes up with another card. The legs and feet are aching and it's got to be circulatory problems. The eyes are deteriorating all the time and what is in good nick doesn't get put to the test as often as it did in the old days or would wish to now. And one of the problems of losing weight is that you get a bony arse and the only thing I can sit on in comfort is a bar stool.

But the crunch is, I suppose, the brain. It's never had more than two or three tracks but they are now in need of repair and like British Rail I shall devote future Sundays to repairing them with Perrier water, the Oxford Dictionary, sackcloth, and ashes. The old nonsense about dying brain cells isn't nonsense. I'm starting a book (I shall bore you with excerpts in the near future) and the difficulty is not being able to remember anything before last Tuesday except for the odd bet, lady, fight and unpaid bill. The fact that my hands tremble indicates no more than a sensitive nature but the fact that my head trembles too has initiated my making another appointment at St Stephen's.

Talking of St Stephen's I must mention the Registrar, Dr McNab, who nursed me through my pneumonic and pleuristic days. I have always held that 99 per cent of the medical profession were, and are, idiots: the playing God with the white coat and talking to you with the sing-song voice as though you were a 12-year-old half-wit. But this man, like the specialist at the Brompton Chest pad, has restored faith. Not often is it that you meet a man you can immediately trust. Very few spring to mind. I can now add Doctor McNab and Collins to the list comprising the first Duke of Wellington, Mr Micawber, Rocky Graziano, Fred Winter, my brothers, my ex-wife Ashley and the breakfast television weather forecaster on BBC. I used to think that you could go into the jungle with my old doctor in Suffolk but he died of drink having told me for five years to abstain.

Yesterday I met a fantastic-looking young woman who looks like a gem but with luck might not be as hard as one. What's extraordinary is that she's a qualified nurse. This is what I've been seeking for years: a beautiful nurse. Matrons I've had basinfuls of but with luck – she loves me, she loves me not – I could end up with my own private drip feed.

115

Just the one

Last Tuesday was as nasty a day as I can remember. I had a bronchoscopy at the Brompton Chest Hospital and it made my eyes water, I can tell you. I was woken up by apprehension at 5 a.m. – the sickening sort I used to feel waiting for the 10.15 from Newbury wondering if they'd taken the buffet car off – and wandered slowly all the way to the hospital pausing at a bench in Hyde Park to smoke some cigarettes, indulge in some self-pity, and attempt an estimate of the number of my days. Wiping the tears from my red, white and blue eyes I strode purposefully on, thinking England Expects and Once more into the breach. I got to the hospital two hours early and sat on the steps smoking more cigarettes.

While I waited in the ward for my pre-med injection a couple of nurses and a young doctor told me so many times that I had nothing to worry about that I knew I had. Above their reassuring smiles their eyes were screaming at the thought of themselves having a bronchoscopy. So they wheeled me off and the pre-med had relieved me of very, very little anxiety. Now this is what happens and doctors need read no further. You're put in a semi-reclining position and the man squirts some anaesthetic jelly up each nostril which really does make your eyes water. Then he sprays your throat with something to dry it up a little, and then it's sprayed with anaesthetic which induced more coughing. Then it's crunchtime. The amazing, reptilian tube with its light at the end is inserted into your hooter. My man had a little difficulty getting through and around the top and a Welsh nurse patted me and said, 'It'll be all right. You've such a small nose, you see. But pretty it is too.' I attempted some facetious jocularity to the effect that small noses didn't mean small everything but, too late, the snake was in my throat. My man, its charmer, now began to take great interest and he repeatedly said to his colleague 'Come and have a look at this', as they stared intently through the other end. Quite obviously there are more navigational problems getting into the lung than I realised. But they were two good men and they told me what was happening all the time. I got one fright. Before getting to the voice box, the one that produced such old immortals as 'I'll Have Just the One', he said, 'I think you've got thrush.' Jesus, that's all I need, I thought, having just discovered Miss Right again. But it was a false alarm.

Then a rather alarming thing happened. He attached a syringe on his end of the line and squirted anaesthetic down. My end didn't like it and tried to reject it. I thought I'd throw up and choke. This he did three times in rapid succession. Then he had trouble in getting into the lung itself – small again, no doubt, in the nurse's opinion – and probably difficult to enter owing to the pub ashtray that's been lodged there for some time. Once in the lung the snake spewed more anaesthetic and I retched and coughed and shook.

The lads were fascinated though and really enjoying themselves. 'See this.' 'What about that?' 'Look at this.' One of them even held my hand, seeing my discomfort. I was rather touched in spite of being busy coughing. Well, they spent what seemed an age looking around the old bellow. More anaesthetic squirts and then something like a thin wire was put down to 'brush' the lung and get a sample of whatever it is that lives on that dreadful, stalagmite-encrusted surface. Then a bit more looking around and chatting and then it was suddenly whipped out of me.

'There we are, all over. It seems to me that you've got a perfectly average lung with maybe some scarring.' Of course, I demanded my money back. What a bloody horrible experience. Then it was almost like handshaking time. 'Well done.' 'You were very good, dear.

Behaved very well you did.' 'Yes, jolly good.' It was rather like being debriefed in an old Ealing film. Perhaps it was the pre-med and all the anaesthetic. I felt like saying, 'I'd like to claim one Me 109 and a possible, sir.' 'Jolly good show, chaps.'

Back in my empty ward I dozed. After three hours or so I thought I'd try a cigarette. Leaning out of the window to avoid detection and still weaker than I realised, I nearly fell out. Now that's a thought. I've never been in traction or an orthopaedic hospital. I might give it a whirl next year.

Settled

Richard Burton overtook me last week but I can assure you that this is only a temporary setback. I have eight years in hand, am cruising into the final furlong hard held and am certain to pip him on the line. All I'm worried about is marrying a Booby. You see I met this strange man last week – he's a racing correspondent – who calls his wife Booby. I asked him why and he told me that the dictionary definition of booby is 'Flightless bird. Ridiculously easy to catch'. Well, I don't like things to be *that* easy. I've worked hard for my four wives – one of them is a *Spare Rib* reader – and I don't eat windfalls. Burton would marry anything as long as it could walk and breathe.

I did, as it happens, meet a possible fifth Mrs Bernard last week but it turns out that she's got the most extraordinary ideas about what's called 'settling down'. This is a very curious phrase used only by women. I have seen feathered birds settling down and I have seen dust settling down and I have even seen bookmakers settling *up* but just quite what women mean by settling down is another matter. I suspect it means that life is no laughing matter. You could have fooled me. But what puzzles me is what on earth did my four wives think they were getting when they married me? It really is a mystery. I mean, you can see a train when it's coming can't you? My fourth wife, who was and is a scrumptious angel, actually said to me, when she called it a day, 'I thought you'd change and settle down.' I wonder if Elizabeth Taylor entertained the same notions about Mr Burton when they first met. Change? Settle down?

What they don't understand is that it takes money to change and settle down. Lawnmowers aren't cheap, you know. Semi-detacheds in Chislehurst don't exactly fall off trees. (Try saying 'semi-detacheds in Chislehurst' after six large ones.) Settling down means giving up eating Wheelers oysters on borrowed money and taking up shepherd's pie. It also means betraying spirits and sycophantising light ale and real ale. Of course, it would be churlish to accuse all women of having settling down syndrome. It's 66-1 against Nell Gwyn ever having told Charles II that she hoped he might change and settle down. (Incidentally, you may not know but Nell Gwyn was found drowned in a shallow stream in Chelsea. Pissed as a pudding, no doubt.) It's also doubtful that Emma Hamilton had these daft notions. Lady Byron on the other hand was a tremendous change-and-settle-down woman and what a ghastly bitch she was.

Now, there are certain conditions in and under which I could change and settle down. I could do it in Antibes with the Queen Mother and I could do it with Cyd Charisse in Barbados. It would entail tremendous sacrifices – I'd miss my hangovers – and I wouldn't be able to look myself in the mirror after having mowed a lawn or washed a car on a Sunday afternoon after helping with the washing-up and changing the odd nappy, but there's no doubt about it, there are ladies I'd give up talking to bailiffs for.

What I'm not quite sure about is whether it's the change or the settling down that's the hardest part. I think I have settled down in so far as I'm pretty set in my ways. I have come to terms with the fact that my dinner is in the oven and always will be. I have also learned to accept the fact that you only get out of life what you put into it. The sagacious prick who informed me of that piece of information would have had his teeth knocked out if I hadn't been in an alcoholic and diabetic coma at the time, but he meant well. And, bless my soul, don't the ladies mean well when they ask you to change and settle down. Never trust people who mean well. Hitler probably meant well and Cromwell certainly hoped we'd change and settle down.

Anyway, I was tremendously flattered when this girl yesterday said to me, 'When I first saw you in the pub I thought to myself, what's that handsome man doing surrounded by rogues?' Apart from her suspect eyesight she's answered her own question, if you see what I mean. Surrounded by rogues. Say no more. But, for her, I'd try to change and settle down. 'Darling, I've asked a few rogues to Sunday lunch. "No knickers" Joyce says she'll weed the border. Maltese Laurie's going to mow the lawn and Charlie says he'll carve the joint. We could play bridge in the evening and perhaps we might splash out on a bottle of sherry.' 'Oh Jeffrey, you're an absolute poppet. I'm so glad you've changed and settled down. You don't miss Soho and all those awful people, do you darling?' 'Of course not, my angel. Take your knickers off. Oops. Sorry. Forgot. We're married and settled down in Chislehurst.'

Privileged

The idea of becoming a writer first came to mind in 1937 when my nanny was pushing me in a superbly upholstered pram across St James's Park on our way to Westminster Abbey for the coronation of King George VI. I was lying there in my ermine nappy sucking on a bottle of Jersey cream – the less fortunate babies of the working and middle classes were sustained on Cow & Gate powdered milk, so mama told me – contemplating my inheritance when it suddenly occurred to me that when I learned to read and write then I'd write. The idea stuck with me for the next ten years right through my preparatory schooldays in Switzerland and I remember vividly, when I was being flown home after having been expelled for climbing Mont Blanc during prep with another boy called Richard West, that the idea came to me to write a novel based loosely on my sexual experiences up to the age of 12.

My next memory of this burning ambition to assault my father's typewriter is of the morning of my 13th birthday. It was a pleasant summer's morning – they started in May in those days – and Jenkins had just handed me a glass of bucks fizz. I had wandered past the fountains, on the lower lawns when I bumped into McGregor, the head gardener. As I plucked an orchid for the buttonhole of my MCC blazer I turned to the grovelling man and said, 'I'm going to be a writer. What d'you think of that?' 'Ee master, tha'll never be a wreeter,' he said. 'Tha moost soofer to wreet.' In spite of his ridiculous accent I continued to listen. 'Tha's too preeveliged,' he continued. 'Why, there's lads oop North who'll wreet reet enough but they's born to it.'

He went on to tell me a remarkable story of three boys of roughly my own age called Alan Brien, Keith Waterhouse and Michael

The good Dr Who. My friend Tom Baker.

Parkinson. Words, McGregor said, flew from their fingers. Brien, he told me, had pulled coal wagons 3,000 ft beneath Durham's pastures when the pit ponies were too exhausted, Waterhouse lived by stealing cigarette cards and selling them to antique dealers from London, and Parkinson earned money for charities by walking to school with no shoes on his feet and only a jam butty to sustain him. Of course, it came as no surprise to me that a mere gardener could impart such information. Rumour had it, below stairs, that McGregor had himself once written a book about a Nottinghamshire coalminer before going to Mexico to have a nervous breakdown with a wretched Hun woman. The fact that in his dotage and obscure retirement he spent most of the time masturbating in the greenhouse endeared him to me somehow. But that is by the by. A mere aside.

I pondered his words as I wandered back to Groomstail. Was it going to be an insuperable hurdle the fact that I wasn't having a deprived childhood? Would it prevent me from writing the novel of the century or getting a staff job on the *Sunday Times*? I determined to consult my confidant Gervase, a young footman my father had found loitering in Hyde Park one night. At that time I spent many hours with Gervase when he was off duty, drinking white ladies in his room with him while I watched him powder his wigs. Ah, what wasted hours! To think at those very moments Benny Green was in Hackney Marshes Public Library memorising the Encyclopaedia Britannica. But, 'tis bootless to exclaim. Soon after, at the start of my first term at Eton, I begged mama to let me walk barefoot to Windsor with a jam sandwich in my pocket but she put her delicate foot down and I was whisked off to Windsor in the Hispana Suiza.

My days at Eton were quite miserable. I had to fag for the school bully, a boy called Colin Welland. He stole my gold fountain pen – surprisingly left for me by McGregor in his will shortly after he was found dead of herpes in the greenhouse – and wrote six television plays with it, although Logie Baird was still perfecting his invention above Bianchi's. The only consolation at Eton was the time I spent punting down the river with Richard West, whom I had bumped into again. We'd drift downstream drinking vodka and White Shield Worthington chasers dreaming of getting staff jobs on national newspapers.

The rest is history. Brien became one of the greatest conversationalists in England since Sheridan, Waterhouse became a great columnist in spite of putting his editor's wife's chihuahua in the fridge at a party when he was drunk one night, and Parkinson became such a wonderful human being he actually disappeared up his own arse and was never heard of again. Poor West went mad and the last I heard he was in Zimbabwe writing a history of the Arts Council. As for me, I spend my days pondering what *might* have been. Once a year I put some flowers on McGregor's grave when I revisit Groomstail, and sometimes I bump into Gervase who's running an afternoon drinking club in Mayfair. For the most part I wish to God I'd suffered a bit more. I'm sure I could have written that book.

Life history

When you get to be 50 you find yourself talking and thinking as much about death and money as you used to about sex. The nearness of one and the shortage of the other fill me with a sense of urgency, but urgency about what I'm not quite sure. I suppose it's a feeling of wanting to *cram* it all in; 'it' being just about everything. I used to leap out of bed at 6 a.m. and get on with the trivialities, now I wake at 6 a.m. and lie there smoking and thinking of these matters until it's time for an analgesic Smirnoff. (That time gets fractionally earlier which is worrying. Why is it perfectly okay abroad?) Anyway, today's heavyheartedness was provoked by good news I had last week. I'm going to start writing a column again for the *Sporting Life* after an absence of twelve years. It won't make me rich but it will be great fun. It seems that my passing out when I was guest speaker at the National Hunt dinner in 1971 has been forgiven. Incidentally, what was odd about that was that no one minded at all except for my boss and trainer, Bill Marshall, who always said to people, 'If you want a really good after-dinner speaker get Jeff. He's not boring because he doesn't say anything.' But, as I say, the heavy heart within is weighty because of the memories of those days on the *Life* between Nijinsky's narrow defeat in the Arc to Mill Reef's victory in the Arc exactly one year later. In fact, just as we were swilling champagne after Mill Reef's victory it was none other than the champion trainer today, Henry Cecil, who told me I'd got the sack from the *Sporting Life*. He'd heard it on the grapevine.

But those 365-odd days were heady, great fun and eventually disastrous for me. To my astonishment the column took off like a rocket and became immensely popular. I wrote a lot about loss and I suppose the average reader could identify with that. There was a ghastly little picture of me at the top of the column so complete and utter strangers recognised me at the races. They'd send me over bottles of bubbly in the Members Bar and trainers who befriended me and showed me the ropes, like Bill Marshall and Eddie Reavey, poured whisky down me like I was a drain. Of course I loved it. To be famous on any circuit in this life is fun and we all want to be loved, don't we. Typical was Ireland. I went to see a trainer called Con Collins one morning and he was on the blower. A maid brought me a tray on which was a bottle of gin, a bottle of whisky and a bottle of brandy. She said, 'Mister Collins will be with you in five minutes. If you need any more to drink ring the bell.' *Any more!* That was just after the first lot had been out, about 9 a.m.

At Newbury one day I won a fair bit on the first race and then started laying favourites to bookmakers and won a little bundle. Risky but beautifully adrenalin-filled days. And the race trains I loved. The restaurant cars filled with bookmakers, spivs, villains, mug punters and scallywags of all kinds playing cards, telling amazing anecdotes about the Turf and drinking as though there was no tomorrow. In those days I think I'm right in saying that the only train in England to sell champagne was the race train to York. We drank the buffet dry by Doncaster. Well, of course, it couldn't last. The whisky was killing me and the bouts of pancreatitis became more frequent.

As I said, the end came at the National Hunt dinner at some dreadful hotel in Kensington. It was suggested that I be the guest speaker and they should have known better. I was extremely nervous, never having spoken publicly before, and I went to the *Life* offices at 6 a.m. to try and write something, couldn't and thought a jar in a Smithfield pub might get the typewriter going. I was accompanied by one of life's and the *Life*'s real eccentrics, a greyhound correspondent called Albert Bright. He used to come out with some very odd remarks and I remember him once saying, apropos of nothing, 'Yes Jeff, I had my first fuck when I was firewatching on the roof of the *Greyhound Express* during an air raid in 1941.' Anyway we got smashed in Smithfield and then continued in the Stab – the *Daily Mirror* pub – at opening time. Still no speech. From there I went to the Colony Room club and so it continued all day. I got to the hotel, fell asleep in the lobby and was taken upstairs and put to bed by the waiters. Here endeth the first lesson.

The next morning I flew to Paris for the Arc de Triomphe and Henry told me I'd been fired. The fact that I could never behave as I did in that year ever again doesn't diminish the depression at the memory of it all. Even at the end the lily demanded gilding. The whisky nudged me into a nervous breakdown and I ended up in a nut house. When I came to, there was an Irish psychiatrist sitting on my bed. Peace and saved at last, I thought. Then he opened his mouth and said, 'What d'you think will win the 2.30?' You just can't win, can you.

Loopy

What people will do to be loved! Dear God. There's a dog in the house I've been week-ending in which got me thinking about it. She eats your shoes and clothes and then, tail wagging, presents you with the remnants as though she's done you a colossal favour. Her eyes plead for reward. That's okay. What isn't is the appalling man I met who balances a wine glass on his head at closing time. He also describes a circle through the air with a glass of beer, the idea being that centrifugal force will prevent a drop of it being spilt. On the occasion I saw this odd plea for love and attention most of the beer went over me. Strangely enough I feel sad that this clown is a member of a dying breed. They're brave enough after all, and I wouldn't fancy having been Will Somers and trying to make Henry VIII laugh all day. But back to the man who balances wine glasses on his head in the hope of a pat on the back.

He's middle-aged, balding, suntanned, well-dressed, cuckolded and deserted, well-spoken, pickled in whisky and wine and he could have been a tea planter in a Somerset Maugham story or maybe a lounge lizard on a pre-war Cunarder. As it is, I see him utterly alone, shuffling downstairs in his slippers in the morning to make a cup of tea with trembling hands and wondering for the millionth time how and why it all went wrong. After the circus-dog-like tricks with the beer – and the wine glass – balancing I finally lost patience with him at an otherwise perfectly lovely garden party. He suddenly leant forward in his deck chair, the white wine sweat pouring down his face, looked at me earnestly and asked, 'Jeff, what do you think life

125

Studying the racing page with John Hurt, the naked civil elephant man, in the Coach & Horses.

means?' I said, 'You're a prick.' What do I think life means indeed! What a bloody stupid question, even from a drunk. Undeterred he went on to tell me, 'You see, I'm a philosopher.'

That went a long way towards explaining why he was dangerously serious and he went on to tell me how his wife had left him. Apparently she got very depressed and only allowed him the leg over once a month (once a year should have been more like it). He suggested she attend a crazy fortnight's seminar on philosophy somewhere, which she did, and when she came back she packed her bags and told him, 'I'm going off to do my own thing.' What a wonderful, meaningless phrase – 'do my own thing'. And serves him right. If I had a wife I wouldn't let her within a hundred miles of a philosopher. Anyway, after the party we went to the pub for more tricks and pleas for attention and at closing time he informed me that 'Life is a dream.' I was sorely tempted to give him a clout over the ear to show him that it isn't but the bell for last orders sounded which also proved it.

The next day he called round to where I was staying and asked my weekend companion if she'd like to go up in an aeroplane for a joy ride. Yes, a philosophical pilot too. 'We can loop the loop,' he said. She was as excited as a 12-year-old boy would be at the prospect of meeting Ian Botham but she asked me did I mind. Well, I did bloody mind but I looked at her lovely face and thought she might just as well get killed in an aeroplane crash as meet Mr Right and bring up four children in Penge or Purley. It also occurred to me that hiring an aeroplane for an hour to loop the loop must be just about the most expensive way man has yet devised to look up a girl's skirt. The loop the loop in Wheelers – bisque to you – is only £1.50 and I've had some good results with it. But they came back in one piece each, she exhilarated and he deeply philosophical, either because it was before opening time or maybe because he'd caught a sight of God up there above Felixstowe. (What a dreadful thing to show a girl. Felixstowe!)

Since then I've tried to be perfectly honest with myself, not delude myself and work out just what it is I do to try and get love and attention. I know I'm not loved for smoking and coughing in bed for an hour every morning so it must be something after opening time. A survey reported in last Tuesday's *Times* said that women like men to be kind and humorous. A survey in next Tuesday's *Times* will doubtless inform us that Queen Anne is dead. That must be it. I did once offer a woman my barstool and it ended disastrously in marriage. I must have told her a joke too on the way to the registry office. But looping the loop is beyond my means and nerves and, anyway, I'm more interested in removing skirts than looking up them. Frankly, I wouldn't have thought aerobatics to be either kind or humorous, but the paths to a girl's heart are not as the crow flies. I shall now retire to the Coach & Horses to balance a glass of vodka, lime, ice and soda on my head and ponder on just whose skirt Icarus was planning to look up.

In a pickle

I read that a member of the General Medical Council has called on his colleagues for quicker identification and treatment for alcoholic doctors. The article, in the *Times*, was headed 'Alcoholic Doctor Tells How He Fought Back'. There are two things that interest me here: first the business of identifying an alcoholic, and secondly the matter of fighting back. How on earth they can have trouble in not identifying an alcoholic immediately, heaven alone knows. I can spot one a mile away. But could they spot my friend Keith I wonder? They must be blind as bats. Anyway, Keith woke up one day sitting in pitch darkness. He groped around for a while and realised slowly that he was in a cinema. Further groping got him to an exit door and he eventually got out on to the street. He didn't know what town he was in but made his way to a pub where, with great embarrassment, he asked the barman where he was. 'Dover', he was told. Then it all came back to him. 'Christ Almighty,' he said. 'I got married yesterday.' I can put the General Medical Council in touch with several Keiths, but I suppose only the 3,000 out of 81,000 alcoholic doctors in this country would be able to identify them quickly.

But we must help the medical profession and give them some clues. A man I know once went to a literary booze-up and walked over to a glass fronted bookcase to see what sort of stuff his host had to read. To his amazement there were no books in the case, only John Raymond standing there in a stupor. I myself once woke up in Cowes of all places and I have even woken up in a drawer at the bottom of a wardrobe. That was fairly frightening. Trying to open a drawer from the inside. It's quite tricky. Then we have our hero on the *Mirror*. I've mentioned him before but, for the benefit of doctors, he is worth recalling. He broke into a pickle factory one night with his girlfriend with the purpose of laying her and fell into a vat of chutney. Then we have the doctors themselves. There were two of them, patients like myself in 1972 in Max Glatt's ward in St Bernard's Hospital. One of them was addicted to barbiturates. He didn't interest me, no drug addicts do, but I asked the alcoholic doctor how did he first know he was an alcoholic and he told me, 'When I sprayed vaginal deodorant on a man's face.'

But the business of the doctor telling how he 'fought back' gets me. I fought back too. I fought back from two and a half years of the most boring, depressing desolation of sobriety you can imagine. I wouldn't go on the wagon again for all the tea in China. For two and a half years I felt apart from the human race. The day I cracked in 1976 I called round to my friend Eva and we cracked a bottle of scotch. Then we went round to the Dover Castle – always full of doctors – and we met up eventually with Frank Norman and drank more scotch. After all those years a bottle of the stuff is damn nigh a killer. Of course it is poison. Frank took me to the Connaught for breakfast the next day and I thought I was going to die. The fact that I'm here now and that Eva and Frank are dead seems unfair.

To go back to the doctors: they apparently consider heavy drinking to be more than four pints of beer a day, or four doubles or a bottle of wine a day. I should have thought that to be the national average lunchtime consumption. But just listen to this. 'I do not remember ever making a mistake, but one of the worst aspects of alcoholism is that you black out. One day I had to ring up the surgery to make sure I had done one of my visits the night before.'

Well, surprise, surprise. What I want to know is, if he blacked out how the hell does he *know* he never ever made a mistake? The wrong leg off? I know I've had the wrong leg *over* because I too have had to ring up the surgery to find out where and if I had done one of my visits the night before. I just don't understand how doctors can be so naive. Well, I do. It's the old business of all the time at school and then in hospital of not seeing anything much of life itself. The Middlesex ought to send their students along to the Coach. They'd find ample opportunity to practise spotting and identifying alcoholics. They're the ones smiling.

Home truths

Most days page three of the *Daily Telegraph* is a haven of sense and sensibility. There's usually something there to remind one that the world is not entirely mad or without some sort of entertainment value. Still, as Frankie Howerd used to say, I suppose one shouldn't mock the afflicted. The trouble is, if you can't mock the afflicted, and obviously this includes one's self, then who the hell can you mock? Anyway, this week's touching tale concerned a woman of 61 who battered her 79-year-old lover to death with a champagne bottle during a sex session at his flat in the South of France. What a way to go. Knowing my luck it would be a bottle of light ale over the nut in a Camden Town bed-sitter. Worse still, it might be a bottle of Perrier over the bonce in a Salvation Army hostel. We must learn to be grateful for small mercies. Anyway, apparently the old man took a new lover, forced his 61-year-old lady into oral sex and she did her nut. Or, to put it more accurately, his nut.

Now, one of the first things to horrify and amuse me about this tragic business is the fact that I've been banking on the supposed fact that once you get to 50 or, say, 60 these aggravations melt away. If I really thought that I'd be crazy for all that nonsense in five years' time I think I'd despair. There's something a little undignified about the behaviour of this couple although the late Mr Hubbers did have the style to keep bubbly by the side of his bed. (Was it vintage I wonder?) I'm an Earl Grey man myself and I wouldn't trust a woman or myself with a bottle in my bed. To be fair to the 61-year-old Cheltenham-Ladies-College-educated Pamela Megginson though, she might well have thought it was only a *half* bottle of champagne. Even so there's something deeply depressing about domestic violence. To this day the slamming of a door fills me with gloom evoking as it does memories of childhood scenes.

And last week at Ascot races of all places I heard of more trouble in the home. I got chatting to a lovely waitress over a lunch hosted by Evelyn de Rothschild and one thing led to another and she asked me if I'd ever been married. 'Not much,' I said. 'You should see my body. It's covered in scars.' 'Really?' she said. 'Well, no not really, but I once was stabbed.' 'That's funny,' she said uncorking yet another bottle of wine, 'I stabbed my husband six months ago.' 'Oh, do tell,' I said, examining the nose of the wine. 'Well, he left me for another woman but he came back three days later when he discovered she couldn't cook. So there I was in the kitchen mashing potatoes and him lying there soaking in the bath and I suddenly thought what a bloody cheek and what the hell am I doing cooking for him so I grabbed a kitchen knife, went into the bathroom and stabbed him.' All I could thing of was what a mess it must have made of the bathwater.

The other thing the champagne bottle case reminded me of was a story about the late Ali Khan I once heard at the races. Apparently he kept a champagne ice bucket by the side of his bed into which he'd plunge his hand to prevent premature ejaculation. Mind you, I don't think an ice bucket over the head would exactly kill you, but caution should be exercised as to what to take into a bedroom. There was the business of the editor and the electric fire a few years back. This man on his wedding night was making love to his bride and got his foot caught in the bars of the electric fire which was at the end of the bed. I don't know that position. Anyway, you can imagine the agony. He went absolutely crazy and started to scream the place down. She, silly cow, came to the conclusion that she was the greatest lover in the world until he started hopping around the bedroom with his smouldering foot. It's nice to know a thing like that about a man when you're asking for a job. (Hacks can send me a stamped, addressed envelope for his name.)

There is an aspect of the champagne case though that does raise a smile of cynicism. I quote Ms Megginson. 'The irony is that I lost control so completely that I destroyed any claim to his estate.' Well, Mr Hubbers might well have been a right bastard, but is it irony, or perhaps agony? He was very good with the handouts until he found another mistress and in the beginning he 'showered' her with expensive gifts and paid her bills at Fortnum & Mason, Simpsons and Selfridges. And some stupid bird on LBC the other morning said women weren't mercenary. But, in the final analysis, I think Pamela Megginson's heart is in the right place. After all, the bottle was empty.

Rum do

Barbados was very much as I left it three years ago: 80 degrees in the shade, humming birds for breakfast companions, the surf whispering along the beaches, too many sickly rum punches – if you could bother to wait twenty minutes for them – and a bit too much Caribbean music. But all quite beautiful. The sun raises the spirits, as do fresh limes, and when the dust settles after ten minutes of tropical rain the exotic flora and fauna of the island seem to vibrate life itself and plunge one into a world of wondrous scents. I even heard a Mozart piano concerto in a hooker's hang-out in Bridgetown one morning but I expect that was a mistake. Anyway, in case anyone should think I have deserted the low life, I should point out that the past ten days were what's called a freebie, courtesy of a PR firm called Infopress and Caribbean Airways. But nothing, of course, is really free and I laundered my way through £200-worth of cocktails, gazing at sunsets, wondering at how odd it was to be doing so with garnishee orders out on me back in London. A double life is the only one.

Our party comprised four women representing the *Sunday Telegraph*, the *Sun, Honey* and *Family Circle*, and proud of it too. We male hacks numbered five, all of whom were appropriately appendaged with feet of clay. Now, in these situations – film locations are similar – geographical changes affect some men strangely. Just as I used naively to deceive myself into thinking that books could be written in the country, most men think that most women can be laid on foreign soil. At least it becomes something of a compulsion to attempt the deed. For my part I detach myself, stand back and watch. No one on the *Sun* could look any better in paradise than they could in Shepherds Bush anyway. So, to our first drama.

One night a very nice bloke indeed arranged a cocktail party in his rooms. Shock, horror, he got drunk. In a fleeting moment of paranoia he told the assembled hacks to fuck off. They did and one of the ladies burst into tears as, of course, any Grub Street lady would do on hearing such appalling language. The next morning at breakfast (orange juice, melon, corned beef hash, poached eggs and more humming birds) our man apologised to the first of the ladies to appear and his apology was greeted by silence. Now, apart from the fact that an apology wasn't really necessary, the high mindedness of a pipsqueak from *Family Circle* was something I couldn't quite take. It rankled all day. By the evening, when it was my turn to get drunk, I expressed my feelings with more unfamiliar four-letter words that Fleet Street hackettes never hear. I also said that I found it odd that ladies earning three times as much as I did couldn't buy a round of drinks, that their assumption – in common with most women – was that all and sundry fancied them something rotten, while I personally thought they were a bunch of slags. I was told later that this sparkling discourse was conducted fortissimo. (Oscar Wilde could have learnt a thing or two at my knee when it comes to calling a woman an old cow.)

What does amuse me in retrospect though is the fact that – so I was later told – our host from the Barbados Tourist Board remained

Francis Bacon in the French Pub.

quite cool and made the understatement of the year when he murmured, 'I suspect a little tension. A possible clash of personalities.' All that really happened was that one of the ladies threatened to slap my face and I warned her that in the event I would be obliged to break her arm.

But it was a jolly good trip and I must advise the Barbados Tourist Board, Infopress and Caribbean Airways that since my return I have plugged Barbados to everyone within listening range, particularly all of my friends who can afford a £1,000-a-week holiday. And, as the same sun sinks in the west over Great Portland Street and not the steel calm of the Caribbean, I find myself wondering did God ever seriously intend that men and women should get on with each other? Do two humming birds make a summer? Is it worth being black to be born in Barbados? Will Bajan Sunshine win the Cesarewitch, as I hope? What on earth can the Tourist Board think of English hacks now? All these imponderables I shall take to my friend, mentor and bank manager, Norman Balon, in whom we trust. The awful alternative, I suppose, would be to take out subscriptions to the *Sun*, *Honey* and *Family Circle*. The world is not yet ready for that, my dear Watson.

Foot fault

Here we are again. This time the Middlesex. St Stephens has lost its appeal for me and the King George V ward here, not to be confused with the George Cinq, has more ambience than the Grenadian-battleaxe-staffed Sir Alfred Tennyson ward in Fulham. Here, tea is served by Malaysian charmers and I'd no more dream of throwing a half pound of butter at them than I would fly or break into a swear. Yes, it's been a ridiculous week. From sublime Barbados to the Middlesex via Bow Street Magistrates Court where I appeared for chastising the staff and one rubber plant in the Raj of India restaurant in Old Compton Street. Fined £10 with £15 damages and suffered one twisted knee getting into a squad car. After I limped out of court I was reminded of a particularly sore left foot. A pebble or a piece of coral on the beach the week before. Nothing much, but the next day my foot was raw, swollen, weeping and painful. Mindful of the diabetic's proneness to gangrene I popped into the clinic where they took one look and then bundled me into bed. I have been occasionally legless but I do like to have *both* feet on the ground.

Not much changes, least of all the medical profession. I was tucked up, put on an anti-biotic drip, X-rayed and God knows what. I lay there waiting for the inevitable first skirmish with the administering enemy. I hadn't long to wait. A young houseman, looking at my records, said, 'You drink and smoke a horrendous amount. Why do you drink?' I thought of saying, 'If you have to ask, then you don't know.' But I replied, 'To stop myself jogging.' I shook my head sadly at him and he got the message. What a silly question. How do these people qualify? Later that evening I was in considerable pain. The infection had swollen the glands in my groin and I asked a female late-duty doctor for some analgesic. She said okay and went off. Forty-five minutes later she returned with two aspirin. I couldn't believe it. She'd be a real wow at the Royal Marsden.

Today my right forearm looks like the treble 20 on a dart board.

Never have I had so many needles stuck into me that missed. But what has amused me until now has been the way that nurses, when they inject or draw blood, always state the obvious. There they are with poised syringe about to plunge and they say, 'Just a little prick.' Half an hour ago when that happened it suddenly occurred to me that that dear nurse might have been referring to me.

Sadly, the patients never ever change. Are they provided by some sort of agency? Is anyone worth talking to ever hospitalised? I fear not. So very awful are the regulars in the day room that I've had to take up smoking in the lavatory again after all these years. *Sun* readers to a man, they stare vacantly at Hungarian children's cartoons all afternoon on the box, occasionally coughing and farting. And to think that is going to be the curtain-down scene for most of us. And, talking of curtains-down, it occurred to me that the last supper menu, quite literally, will be brown windsor soup and minced beef with cabbage and boiled potatoes. But no expense is spared when it comes to food. Even the ice-cream is sent up in the hot wagon. It would be a crime to cut back or destroy any of this and the dreadful Norman Fowler's ears should be burning. If they fell off I doubt whether any of the doctors or nurses here would care a jot. They're rightly upset. Perhaps I'm biased, but these people keep coming to my rescue. Yes, they hate Fowler and I fear we may have to learn how to come to our own rescues.

P.S. Fleet street colleagues seem to have their wires crossed. When I mentioned last week the harridans who accompanied me to Barbados I did not mean to include the delightful lady from the *Sunday Telegraph*. She was fun and got her shout. As in *Macbeth* there were only three witches in Barbados.

Last resort

We were idly wondering what on earth Watneys will do to the French pub when Gaston Barlemont retires. Piped accordion muzak à la Maigret? Barmaids with red, white and blue aprons and caps? Fitted carpets? God save us. In no time at all there will be nowhere to go, and what's more I read in the *Telegraph* that the sun will snuff out in 5,000 million years' time. I give Soho about another five years and I have a very uncomfortable feeling that I might survive it. The trouble is that there aren't many worthwhile villages left in London. I used to have a fondness for Marylebone High Street when I lived there but it's far too bland and benign. Chelsea seems to consist of nothing but shops which sell jeans, people too young to talk to and failed faces too embarrassing to look into. I haven't got the socialist wardrobe obligatory for drinking in Hampstead – woollen tie, corduroy trousers and tweed jacket – and the fact that I was born in the wretched place, had my first experience of sex on the Heath and my first liver biopsy in the Royal Free doesn't justify loitering in the Flask watching people pay homage to John Hurt, who was a nice chap before he became a naked civil elephant man.

Fleet Street you can keep. I've had enough dealings with solicitors not to want to drink with them in El Vino and, weighed down as I am by a quantity of chips on the shoulder and an innate bitterness, nor do I want to talk shop with hacks who earn £20,000 a year for putting in an appearance to write 300 words a week. There was a time, would you believe, when Notting Hill Gate swung a little. I had a fight with Roy Campbell in a pub there on my 18th birthday and nearly every day was a party day when the Roberts, Colquhoun and McBryde, had a studio in Bedford Gardens. George Barker also livened things up and John Minton subsidised the drinks to a certain extent. Later, in the Sixties, the vision of Sally Vincent must have depressed the female populace of Notting Hill.

The place I can see making something of a comeback is north of Soho – its old annexe, Charlotte Street. Unpolluted by sex shops, dirty bookshops and strip clubs it still has a certain charm. The fact that the denizens of the Duke of York, the Wheatsheaf, the Black Horse and the Fitzroy are mostly dead doesn't mean it couldn't be re-populated. I can also see Islington gaining in popularity, although there are far too many people living there with tenuous connections and pretensions to the 'arts'. A lot of people in Islington have been hinting at potential talent for at least fifty years. Most of them end up as rip-off antique dealers feigning an understanding of culture which in reality is materialised by a discussion about nuclear disarmament at a wine and cheese party and by their revolting children.

In spite of being a Londoner, the City remains a mystery to me. But there must be some good men there. Britain is Great Britain because the majority of the people who run the Stock Exchange, like those who hold the reins in the House of Commons, are permanently

Frank Norman, David Warner and Eva Johansen at a Derby Day party in my flat, 1975.

drunk. So I presume there must be a few good dives there although I only know Sweetings and a revolting pub opposite Liverpool Street Station packed with lager-swilling travelling salesmen. Women do seem scarce in the City though. I suppose they must be manning the typewriters most of the time. Women are very important to a village, and if saying so gives offence it is only because I am unlucky enough to be a male heterosexual. This has caused a lot of interference to the smooth running of my life. Nevertheless I like to see the odd sex object over the rim of my glass. And that's one reason for not drinking in the village of Mayfair or in the Grays Inn Road, where only very important people from the *Times* and *Guardian* drink.

No, when Soho dies it might even mean moving out of London altogether. But where to? I could never live in a village proper again because of the necessity of driving. Brighton, Bristol and Cambridge have occurred to me as possibilities and although I gather from my colleague Michael Heath that Brighton is almost 100 per cent homosexual it does have a school of journalism which might be useful and possibly lead to a job on the *Sun*. We can all dream.

Meanwhile I sit by the bedside of dying Soho holding her hand but wondering wouldn't it be kinder to switch off the life-support system. When the likes of my brothers, Tom Baker and Conan Nicholas, who gave the world cat racing, stop frequenting Soho then it will be time to charter that bus which is going to drive us over Beachy Head. Book your seat now. There's only room for 52.

Dessert Island

The business of being shipwrecked on a desert island is something that has intrigued me ever since Roy Plomley started his radio programme *Desert Island Discs*. I've thought of the people I'd like to take, and those I'd hate to, and I seem to remember vaguely having written about them in this column. What came to mind the other day was desert-island food and it's a tricky business choosing twenty-one meals assuming you're going to eat breakfast, lunch and dinner every day. At first, what sprang to mind was cordon bleu, haute cuisine, provençale and all the sort of stuff that the likes of Bernard Levin drool over. But this excludes some of the great dishes of the world that have gone unrecorded by fatty Carrier and the great Elizabeth David. Consider the bacon sandwich washed down by a pot of 1983 Lyons Orange Label tea sipped from a bone china cup (mugs are for cocoa only). I prefer my bacon in the white sandwich loaf bread that's supposed to be so bad for you – wholemeal bread detracts from the bacon flavour – and there should be just a hint of brown sauce. And what about that prince of left-overs, bubble and squeak? As a child, my favourite meal was Sunday supper. Cold lamb left over from lunch with pickles and bubble and squeak fried gently to a golden brown on the outside.

I could not eat à la Gavroche or L'Etoile twice a day every day. I could eat Chinese and Indonesian food nearly every day. Indian once a week and certainly a paella, just about my favourite dish, once a week. A funny thing about paella is that I've never had a really good one in Spain. I've had plenty of rice concoctions that were the consistency of porridge, but I suspect that you have to go to a three-star job in Madrid to get the real McCoy. Taste apart, it's great fun to make a paella if you've got a couple of hours to spare and I have most days. It isn't, by the way, necessary to cook everything in a paella together. Ingredients can blend just as effectively just before serving. I suppose you might call shepherd's pie a sort of English equivalent of paella and it's an obligatory weekly desert-island dish although it has fallen into disrepute in recent years thanks to the ever declining standards of British pub food. I once stood in for a chef in a pub off St Martin's Lane who'd fallen ill and my friend and guvnor asked me to make a large shepherd's pie. I used steak tartare mince for the foundation and a bottle of 1949 Châteauneuf-du-Pape to bolster the gravy. It was quite stupendous, sold like hot cakes and the guvnor lost about £6 on the dish. The next day I devoted my time in the kitchen to preparing that old classic, the Beethoven's Fifth of food, bangers and mash. Again the guvnor and I nearly fell out. I took a taxi to Jermyn Street to Paxton's for the sausages and he raised both eyebrows when I put egg yolks and cream into the mash. Mashed potatoes must be whipped and not just pulped.

Ill health forces me to eschew most puddings but I do like apple pie and fresh fruit salad. What I would want plenty of on this wretched island is ice cream. Where this could be flown in from, God alone knows. I know of only three places in London: Marine Ices, the one next to Goodge Street tube station and the new one whose name I've also forgotten in Battersea. A word of warning here about ice cream. Never eat the popular brands. I once worked nights as a packer in the most famous establishment and I saw them add left-over fat from their sausages to the ice cream. I also once saw a lunatic urinate into a vat of ice cream.

Another gastronomic must would have to be the weekly injection of fish and chips. Although it's necessary to travel to France to get properly cooked chips, efforts are being made here in some brasseries. For the most part English chips are too fat and soft and remind me of fried cotton wool. Even Wheelers haven't got the hang of them. What amuses me in that restaurant are the faces of people when they see me anointing my fish and chips with tomato ketchup. I gather from their toffee noses that ketchup is frightfully infra dig. And speaking of fish I would like kedgeree once a week for breakfast.

I think what I might miss on this island is the hassle, rudeness and aggression I seem to experience in Indian and Chinese restaurants. But I'm sure Man Friday could be trained to get hysterical when I try to pay by cheque having lost my cheque card. He could bang my plates – palm leaves – down in front of me and then sneer at my tip. On second thoughts I think I will get a friend with an expense account to take me to the Connaught as soon as possible.

Rover's return

I took myself away from the well-beaten track last week and dilly-dallied in Chelsea for a couple of days. It's well known that the Kings Road died some years ago when it was taken over by jeans shops and so-called trendy young people obsessed by pop music, but the cancer is spreading. There isn't a pub or restaurant in the entire street worth going to, with the possible exception of the Man in the Moon, which is physically a very pretty pub. Further north the Fulham Road isn't quite so bad. At least it's populated in the main by middle-aged people whose world-weariness is such a refreshing change from the youth who think that entertainment consists of throwing bread rolls at each other over dinner.

But the Fulham brigade, centred mainly in the Queen's Elm, Finches and the Chelsea Arts Club, are an extraordinary bunch, all of them caught in a sartorial time warp. Most of the men are greying, wear roll-neck jerseys, jeans and desert boots and you know damn well they sculpt or paint and have just missed the boat in both departments. The more solvent ones probably have teaching jobs, studios and common-law wives they first beheld in a life class. Fulham must be the last outlet for manufacturers of corduroy. The place is also chock-a-block with women painters and I think they're very brave considering that what women are far and away the best at is writing novels. They are so good at it in fact that I find it slightly uncanny. Alice Thomas Ellis says it's like playing with dolls' houses. You move people from room to room and wonder what you're going to do next with them. Another strange inhabitant of the Fulham Road is the man who supports Chelsea or Fulham football club and who you'd think would have more intelligence than to do so. There's an awful sort of snobbery about football, and local thespians and television persons suffer from it the most.

But, when all's said and done, the strip 'twixt the Arts Club, Queen's Elm and Finches is still one of the better villages of London.

140

Mirror Group Newspapers Limited

Holborn Circus London EC1P 1DQ
Switchboard 01-353 0246
Direct Line 01-822 3 544

Telegrams Mirror London EC1
Telex 27286

11 July 1975

Mr Jeffrey Bernard
39 Nottingham Place
W.1.

Dear Mr Bernard,

I read with interest your letter asking for information as to your behaviour and whereabouts between the years 1960-1974.

On a certain evening in September 1969, you rang my mother to inform her that you were going to murder her only son.

If you would like further information, I can put you in touch with many people who have enjoyed similar bizarre experiences in your company.

Yours sincerely,

MICHAEL J MOLLOY

Registered Office Holborn Circus London EC1
A Company registered in England (No 168 666)
and a subsidiary of Reed International Limited

I have some pleasant memories of it anyway. The 'Master', as we used to call the poet George Barker, kindly gave me my first experience of amphetamine in the Queen's Elm when I was 18 and I once worked behind the bar there for the guvnor, Sean Treacy, who very understandingly one evening gave me five minutes off to hit one of his more boring customers. The Anglesea down the road has fallen off disastrously, being full as it is of Hooray Henrys, but you can catch a glimpse from it sometimes of Miss Ava Gardner walking her dog. I did live there once, albeit under the enormous thumb of a paranoically jealous woman who thought I'd been to bed with someone even when I popped out for five minutes to buy some cigarettes – five minutes! I ask you – but I'd quite like to return to the area had I £1 million to buy a flat. As it is, the disgusting Soho is a mere twelve minutes walk away and Soho is going to become even more disgusting soon. A sure sign of Gaston Berlemont's imminent retirement from the French pub is that he called in the £20 I owed him last week. I think we can all guess just how Watneys will refurbish the place.

Which reminds me. The Queen's Elm, the French pub and the Coach & Horses were the only pubs I came across during the festive season which did *not* have any Christmas decorations. A very good sign indeed. The *printed* card wishing all its customers a happy Christmas, either in shop window or pub, is a shabby hypocrisy, as is the ill-disguised advertisement on scaffolding announcing that McAlpines apologise for any inconvenience to the public. Bollocks. But, as I say, the contemplation of London villages has become something of a permanent fantasy. Charlotte Street has a lot to recommend it, good shops and activity, but with sufficient loot I could settle for spending the rest of my life in a hotel, preferably Browns or the Ritz. I'm very fond of room service and in the Park Lane Hilton you can get more than a chicken sandwich and a drink sent up to your room. In the Shelbourne Hotel in Dublin the staff have real wit and cunning. I'd just moved in there one day and was having a clean up in the bathroom – stop me if you've heard this – when a little bell hop knocked on the door and squeaked, 'Mister Bernard, I've a message for you.' I shouted out, 'Slip it under the door.' 'I can't, sir,' he said, 'it's on a salver.'

Eye contact

I keep getting bombarded with unsolicited mail. More often than not it's publicity rubbish from Channel 4 which should be going to Richard Ingrams, the humorist and television personality. This morning I received an invitation to a preview of something called *Pictures of Women – Sexuality.* The blurb goes on to say, 'Women today are limited and defined by sexuality in ways that men are not. Starting from this premise, a production team called Pictures of Women has fashioned six programmes asking why this situation has arisen and looks, from a woman's point of view, at its effects on a wide range of contemporary social issues.' Etc, etc, Bla, bla. 'The series examines the nature of sexual attraction, pornography, sex in advertising, prostitution, sexual harassment at work and the continuing limits to sexual equality.' Then, at the foot of the page, 'Refreshments will be served after the screening.' *After?* I ask you. Not only after but the wretched preview itself starts at 11.30 a.m., by which time I will have already been hard at work in the Coach & Horses for half an hour. What's more, you'd need a skinful to sit through this sort of film.

But what's really been getting up my nose for the past five or six years is the revolting way women take sex and themselves so bloody seriously. The fact that so very few of them do so is little consolation to me since, being a hack, I'm permanently surrounded by those very few or, at least, a large proportion of them. I used to have a soft, and occasionally hard, spot for Germaine Greer, but just see how fame destroys people. It's awful. With a Booker Prize she'd be certifiable. But I wonder, does the business of taking sex so seriously have anything to do with the fact that so few women can bear to own up simply to liking it very much? And just what is the problem concerning prostitution? The expense. If any reader knows of a call girl who accepts Barclaycard I'd be grateful to be informed of her name and address. (My new Barclaycard arrived this morning. The old one was cut in half by a shop assistant in the Victoria Wine Shop in Berwick Street in front of six other customers. That was far more serious than sex.) What I do think is utterly rotten is the business of 'No Knickers' Joyce, who told me that one of her customers paid her by cheque and then stopped it. Not cricket.

But the business of sexual harassment in the office is, I think, slightly exaggerated. I have, would you believe, been on the other end of it. Fifteen years ago, at the *Daily Mirror*, there was a secretary who couldn't type for crying over me. It got on my tits as well as the boss's but I suppose tits is a sexist word in spite of the fact that men have them – of a sort – too. But I'm all for sexual equality. When I was in Moscow I can't tell you what pleasure it gave me to watch women shovelling concrete on building sites. I don't like watching them write very much, they have such a facility for it, but I do like to see them work. Sadly, I know only three equal women, Irma Kurtz, Sally Vincent and Hazel Evans, all of whom generously stand their round. Oh yes, and my landlady and Liz Elliot at *Private Eye*. As for pornography the worst thing I can say about it which women will be totally unaware of is that it's ruined Soho. My heart bleeds for the low life café society that's been taken over by dirty bookshops and strip clubs.

143

But you note that this film examines the nature of sexual attraction. What is there to examine? Speaking as one whose life has been totally ruined by falling in love with the packaging and not the woman I find it pretty hard to believe that women don't want to be sexually attractive. Of course, I'm in the wrong business and owning a typewriter as opposed to a cosmetic or high-heeled-ankle-strap-shoe factory is a pretty grim financial alternative. And speaking of sexual attraction, the most extraordinary thing has happened to me. I've become totally besotted by the woman who works in the optician's shop I go to – I keep losing my glasses. It's really quite pathetic. I keep going into the shop on the slightest pretext. It's horribly like being 16 again. She's not what you'd call a knockout but I fancy her almost to the point of obsession and I'd very much like to be paid by Channel 4 for talking about the problem on television. Last week I went into the shop three times to have my glasses tightened and when she puts them on my head she has to stand very close to me. I fear this could lead to six months in Wandsworth. What I do know is enough about women to be sure that she spends an age every morning making herself attractive to the likes of idiots like me. But I can't go on and on having my eyes tested just to be near her. I would be extremely grateful to any female reader of this column who could tell me of an effective and new verbal opening gambit. I fear she can read an awful history book in my eyes.

Bedfellows

I must be mellowing a little. I can no longer dislike doctors as I used to. Perhaps, at last, I'm too old for them to play God in a white coat to. But for the rest, the Bosch and Brueghel patients, the boils and burst veins, the dentures in glasses, the stumps that twitch remembering old legs, the hideous humiliation of the sick – all is grotesque. Patients are, for the most part, pretty disgusting and sickness reveals the man of straw and not so much of the nobility I've read about for years.

To my left lies Major Saunders, clinging on to the 'Major' nearly forty years after the event. He has circulatory problems and his purple toes are gnarled and twisted and you could probably pick them

Punch

23-27 TUDOR STREET, LONDON EC4Y 0HR

Telex LDN 263263 (Unipapers) Telephone: 01-583 9199

Jeffrey Bernard
c/o Private Eye
34 Greek Street
London W 1   Nov 23 1977

Dear Jeffrey,

Are you going to do the fucking article or aren't you ?

yours

Miles

Miles Kington

PUNCH PUBLICATIONS LTD. Directors: A V Caudery N A Whinfrey W Davis B P Knox-Peebles R Tookey R E Forrester
Registered office: 23-27 Tudor Street London EC4Y 0HR Telephone: 01-583 9199 Registered in England No. 797363

off his feet like plums from a tree. Without a batman and wife he is lost. A frightened man – I've watched him at meal times and I think he's actually frightened of meat. Opposite the Major there lies Mr Lawrence, a post-office worker minus one gall bladder. Yesterday the tetchy Major asked Mr Lawrence where he lived, and when he was told in St John's Wood, near Lord's, the Major said, 'Oh. Are you a member?' I am surrounded by spite. The fourth man who makes up our quartet is Mr Wright who has had a very nasty operation indeed. Sadly it has left him anally fixated. Every day he buttonholes someone to recount to them the story of his greatest and most satisfactory movement ever. The memory of that one moment is all he has left. If only the medical wards weren't full I wouldn't have to endure these surgical cases.

But the amputees are both jolly men even though, as they're fond of telling me, they do happen to be grim warnings to any diabetic. Mr Thompson has one leg and Mr Davies none. Thompson says his gangrene was the result of fifty cigarettes a day which closed up his veins. A doctor overhearing this said, 'It's no use telling Mr Bernard. What he closes up with fifty cigarettes he then opens with vodka.' Being alive is a constant source of irritation to the medical profession. Or, at the very least, an okay liver-function test proves that the patient isn't getting his just deserts.

But worse than this quartet are the ladies along the corridor. There is an ancient Glaswegian pug dog, and a tart with a rose-coloured silk dressing gown, dyed red hair and colossal sunglasses and they spend all day on the landing by the lifts – the only place we are allowed to smoke – talking to a Greek toad, poor woman, who is waiting for her husband to die. They try to converse in mime, sign language or just by talking very slowly as though that will itself open up the mysteries of language. The tart constantly asks, 'What is Greek for cancer?' and is told 'Athens. Very good. Very pretty.' 'And how is your husband today?' 'Athens. Very good.' Then she starts crying again.

What we have got here though are some fine tea-ladies and bottle-washers. The days of those old naval actions against the dreaded Santisima Trinidad at St Stephens are over, thank God. Here we are looked after by ladies from Manila and Singapore. Mere junks bobbing harmlessly up and down at their moorings in the kitchen. You wouldn't put the Middlesex into the Hospital Good Food Guide, but it must go into the Hospital Good Physician and Surgeon Guide. My houseman, a spectacular Indian woman, is seething with self-confidence and that's always good in a doctor. The only other people here with the same measure of it are the duo with one leg between them. But then it's *fait accompli* and I suppose they haven't much alternative but to be brave. The Major could learn from them. He's at this moment toying with some macaroni cheese which won't bite him back. How *did* we win the war?

Shop-soiled

As you may well imagine, the farmer's wife who is about to inherit £3 million has been on my mind this past week and I'm very pleased to hear that she does *not* intend to change her way of life. Quite right. She did after all have to fly home from a skiing holiday to consult her solicitors; it's not as though she had to walk back from Butlin's Holiday Camp at Skegness to consult them. So why change? The farm must be worth a few bob too, what with land fetching – I'm guessing – something in the region of £1,000 an acre. So why change all that? What she might like to change is her husband, mind you, and a windfall like this could well keep him on his toes for a while. Poor bastard. I feel sorry for him. What a colossal cosh to be under. In fact, if I was him I'd leave her. He'll only have to lower his copy of *Farmer's Weekly* at the breakfast table to give her a dog-like look of affection, his tail so to speak wagging the while, and she'll snap, 'Who the hell d'you think you're looking at, you poxy little creep?'

Anyway, obviously I've done a little fantasising, and not for the first time, on the question of what I'd do with serious loot. And what it comes down to is, quite simply, I'd spend it. I wouldn't change. It's far too late for that and I wouldn't go mad because I've tried that too and I didn't like it a lot. What would change, I'm afraid, are my friends and acquaintances. I'd hate to see their embarrassment. And women in general? Would they only then suddenly see what's been standing, longing and trembling for mere crumbs, in front of them for the past thirty years? You can bet on it and I'd adore to be loved for my money. Especially over Sunday lunch in the Tour d'Argent.

But these silly dreams don't last long, thank heavens, because I'm fairly contented, and what banished the £3 million from my mind was something I thought of wandering down the Kings Road on my way to the Queen's Elm for the third time in one week. (Where are you Tom Baker?) What I saw opposite the Town Hall was an establishment called the Reject Shop. Now it struck me, like a punch between the eyes, that if you – I mean me of course – stood in the window for a while you might actually get bought by someone quite nice. I mean obviously some people – my ex-wife for example – would walk past and sneer, but you never know your luck. The idea really tickles my fancy. I see myself in a sleazy afternoon club in the Shepherds Market area being introduced by my tarty, blonde purchaser – her bust trying to burst out of her angora jersey, a drop of gin slowly sliding down her chin, her handbag open and full of cosmetic chaos – to her jaded lounge-lizard friends. 'Got him in the Reject Shop in Chelsea. Not bad for 20 quid. Couldn't get it up, mind you, when I first took him home, but it's amazing how he comes to life when you pour a couple of vodkas into him. Have another, dear.'

I can think of many people who could and should be put in the window of the Reject Shop. Edward Heath limped to mind when I first thought about it but what would you want to buy him *for*? Taki's friends would, I think, make a pretty interesting display but, come to think of it, I *am* in a bloody reject shop and have been for years. I suppose a sort of refusal to be gift-wrapped might have been my downfall. But if you've got a few bob and like a dog around the house then I can introduce you to several possibilities. There are dogs here that will sit up on their hind legs and beg, fetch you your *Sporting Life*, lick your boots and stay loyal for a day at a time. Someone I don't want to see in my reject shop is the smocked and pitchfork-holding farmer who'll be gone with the wind after the wife's windfall.

Fireworks

I went out last Sunday to celebrate the anniversary of Byron's birthday – excuses, excuses – and someone transferred me from the Queen's Elm to the Chelsea Arts Club for lunch. All very jolly. But you may imagine my amazement, while I was being signed into the club, to see that the doorman was reading Henry James. I once had an account with Coutts in the Strand and the commissionaire used to stand in the doorway doing the *Times* crossword. I sense a revolution coming. Years ago, in 1952 to be exact, I was threatened with a beating up in Hanley Deep pit when I took my 'snapping' down to the coal face wrapped up in the *Times*. An angry collier asked me was I 'a fuckin Tory?' and I inadvertently made matters worse by saying no and that I only got the *Times* for the crossword and the cricket and racing. (What the hell I still get it for God knows.) I'm an addict I suppose. But the sight of Henry James, even in paperback, is not conducive to a pissy luncheon. I find reading Henry James akin to self-flagellation. Somewhere, I suppose, there strolls a traffic warden reading Proust between accepting bribes from Rolls Royce owners. If these people really want a laugh to alleviate the boredom of their menial tasks I suggest they turn to S.J. Perelman or the ace of black jokers, Alice Thomas Ellis.

But the biggest laugh I had last week was the one I found in the pages of the *Standard* which concerned the lady who had an affair with a tramp. It seems that a rich German bird, Gabrielle Burchard, met an eccentric tramp, Godfrey Taunton, felt sorry for him and then fell in love with him. When he gave her the elbow she found him asleep one night in Holland Park, poured petrol over him and set him ablaze. Of course, our tramp is a former public schoolboy. It gets better. In a statement to the police she said, 'I wanted to keep him. I was getting more interested in him and took him home. He just sat and sewed patches for hours. I went to bed. When I woke he was kneeling by the bed. He said. "Wake up, it is breakfast time." I noticed something on my mattress. It was a dried rose from the dustbin.' Then she went on to say that the patchman told her he hadn't had sex for years and that then they went through the ordeal five or six times.

Well, the whole affair makes me feel tremendously grateful to the handful of ladies I've spurned. I've received abusive and obscene letters, been hit and had drinks thrown in my face, but not yet been set on fire in the physical sense. I would guess that the rose from the dustbin was the final straw. Even I once bought the entire stock of a flower shop for my ex-wife when I was wooing her. Admittedly it was 4.30 p.m. and they'd nearly sold out, but you have to make an effort. Mind you, there's no gain-saying that five or six leg-overs for a dustbin rose is very good value indeed and any man who can shoot a line as witty as 'wake up, it's breakfast time' deserves what he can get even if it does end in a blazing row.

Anyway, it all ties in with an old friend I met in the Queen's Elm before the Henry James lunch in the club. You wouldn't have guessed that I've played Cupid, but I have. Years ago, my vaguely look-alike mate walked into the Elm and a woman jumped up and screamed at him, 'You shit,' and flung a drink in his face. He said words to the effect, 'What's all that about?' and she said, 'You're that bastard Jeff Bernard.' He explained that he wasn't and she apologised. Then they got talking, fell in love and they've been happily married ever since, their union being blessed with two children. I still live in hope of some woman leaping to her feet, hurling vodka in my face and screaming, 'You're that shit Paul Newman', but I fear it may never come to pass. There was another drink-throwing episode in the Queen's Elm years ago too when I brought two people together. A married couple were having a gritted-toothed row and the wife suddenly threw a pint of bitter in his face. He ducked and I derived the full benefit of it in my face and down my suit. They laughed so much they made it up and got together again. Whether they're still together I don't know. As the patchwork tramp will tell you, where there's smoke there's fire.

Master class

In recent years I seem to have had the somewhat dubious good fortune to attract the occasional gerontophile. It is my friends and acquaintances who consider it to be my good fortune while it is I who consider it a dubious and inevitably disastrous form of coarse angling. What they overlook while they're smirking and saying 'I don't know what she sees in a geriatric old twit like you. She's only 24. She'll kill you', is the ghastly role I end up playing which is that of the teacher. Yes, believe it or not, but for about two months of the year every year I end up being the guru of Great Portland Street. Unhampered as I am by a deep and heavy intellect – I can no longer understand Germaine Greer – I find myself continually plucking and rescuing young ladies from the suburbs and provinces, giving them a glimpse of my Aladdin's Cave, turning their heads with the sights and sounds therein and then being rejected for someone younger when they've had their fill of this old fool's fancies.

The times I've cooked splendid meals for young ladies, introduced

With Lester Piggot.

them afterwards to Mozart and other friends in the sitting room, lent them books in hard covers, taken them out to meet the lions of Fleet Street, Newmarket and Shaftesbury Avenue, stroked them in every way, converted them from bran to grain products, switched their allegiance from the Beatles to Beethoven, from rock to romance, given them every sort and kind of kiss of life only to see them disappear down a rabbit hole with an advertising executive in a sports car are legion. Last year, there was the 24-year-old nurse. Now I'm well aware that at my age it's a lifeboat and not a dreamboat that I need but I must admit I found her initial interest in me quite irresistible. In no time at all I had her eating expertly with chopsticks, caught her in the bath one morning humming the Waldstein, introduced her to Ascot, Richard West, Lester Piggott, french dressing, taxis and Stolichnaya and there's very little else you can do for a girl apart from make her unhappy and, of course, I got around to that. I ended up snapping. I don't mean cracking up emotionally. I mean snapping like, 'And what the fuck do you know about David Hockney, you stupid bitch.' And that was bad. You shouldn't frighten people, if for no other reason than that they never forget or forgive fear. And perfect fear driveth out all love.

Only once, and quite recently, has the boot been on the other foot and I've played the pupil. I had a fascinating dalliance with a girl who was studying philosophy at London University. She had such a profound effect on me that I didn't actually give up smoking, but I managed to do without the post-coital cigarette for a while (the ones that are obligatory in all BBC television plays.) I used to lie there staring at the stains on the ceiling, my left hand cupped around her right breast, while she told me about Leibniz, Kierkegaard, Schopenhauer and Wittgenstein. This was a lot better than the boredom of having actually to plough through the wretched books, and it put me in mind of the delightful affair years ago in Suffolk when I used to snuggle up to the vicar's daughter's warm bum as she told me about Martin Luther. I think I preferred both experiences to that of my most recent tutorial I gave under the duvet to a drama student on the subject of why Lester Piggott is worth 7 lbs, or nearly three lengths, more than any other jockey in the world at Epsom.

Yes, this new drama student, a leggy filly with bags of scope for future development, is an interesting enrolment at the Great Portland Street Academy for Young Women. What I'm trying to figure out though is just why anyone has to go to school to study drama. I study it every day from the moment I get up, check up in the mirror as to my existence and then open the mail. This isn't going to last long either. It's difficult to teach a young bitch new tricks. She's a nail-biting nutter. The word neurotic, like the word 'nice', is overused and misused but I know what *I* mean by it. Neurotic girls are sexually tractable but prone to overact at the end of act three. (The 1983 nurse actually had the gall to come into the Coach & Horses the other day to take a curtain call.) No, I can't take any more of these private master classes. This summer I'm negotiating to rent somewhere like Dartington Hall where I and some of my friends can give a summer school. Young women wishing to enroll for the week's course should report to me with £500 in cash, a toothbrush, seven pairs of clean knickers, seven boxes of Kleenex and an open if not actually blank mind. There will be several lectures and some well-known old classics including Geoffrey Wheatcroft's 'Legless in Gaza', Cosmo Landesman's 'Premature Ejaculation: A Blessing in Disguise', my own humble offering, 'Getting the Most out of your Nervous Breakdown' and an interesting talk by Richard West, illustrated with lantern slides, on how Albert Schweitzer discovered the missionary position. There will be a licensed bar, a little night music and all confidences will be respectfully betrayed. On the last night there will be a ball. Jill Tweedie will decide whose when the time comes.

Rubber plants

It's been another rather silly week in the back garden of Soho. On Monday I met a black bird with thrush and, as I predicted in last week's column, the drama student didn't last long. Lingering over a pot of Earl Grey at the end of an afternoon seminar – included in the service charge – she casually dismissed King Lear as being an old man with woman troubles. I was so irritated I asked her to remove her toothbrush from my bathroom beer mug and make other arrangements for her future unhappiness. Such people come here in taxis but leave in buses and it serves them right. Well, later that evening – back at the drawing board so to speak – in Kettners and sipping Cointreau, the poor man's pre-frontal lobotomy, these tired old eyes came to rest on this delightful-looking black bird who omitted to tell me that she had thrush until I had actually signed her into the Great Portland Street Academy. I've put her on a crash course of natural yoghurt which rather messily has to be applied to the parts as well as swallowed and I've sworn her to celibacy until the start of the flat racing season which opens at Doncaster on 22 March, exactly one day after J.S. Bach's birthday. You could now call her a bird in the bush and I fear I have none in the hand. The next morning I perked up a bit when the telephone rang and I heard the soft voice of my Dublin bookmaker. He told me that Capture Him, held in the highest esteem by his trainer Vincent O'Brien, must be backed when he comes to England in the spring and possibly for the 2,000 Guineas, but that's by the by and I only mention it since the information comes from the same source that gave us Bajan Sunshine for last year's Cesarewitch.

At lunchtime, Charlie took me to a rather superior fish-and-chip shop where they gave us some tepid white wine in teacups after hours. They meant well, but it was quite disgusting. Wheelers have got it right. If you make it cold enough you can drink Chateau filth without noticing it. Anyway, the plonk went to my head and I ordered a suit I can't pay for on my way home. Which reminds me. The Inland Revenue finally got me to court last Friday and they're going to tap my income at source for the next 13 months. I think I slipped up badly. I made the wretched collector an offer which he accepted with such alacrity that I knew immediately I'd gone over the top. Can you imagine writing something like sixty columns for practically nothing? So, if I sound a little churlish here until next year's Grand National you'll know it has nothing to do with thrush or drama students. I managed to needle the collector though. What these people don't like or understand after you've been pleading poverty in the dock is one's hailing a taxi outside the court instead of jumping on a bus. That's why they're tax collectors who'll never know the invigorating joys of treading water in the deep end without a life belt.

But something will turn up and a bit did on Thursday. An extremely shrewd television producer called round in the morning and asked me if I'd like to go on the box and talk about the low life, how I got into it and why I like it. Now, for three minutes that would be something of a doddle but this man says it's for 28 minutes straight into a camera. Twenty-eight bloody minutes! If the film doesn't end up in the cutting room dustbin I want you to watch it – I'll tell you the date when I know it – to see how a person can destroy themselves with their own vanity. It's something I've always wanted to do and it will probably turn out to be as farcical as my courtroom appearances. Every time I go to court I expect to see the famous titter go around the court. I think I'm going to be as witty as Oscar Wilde and have everyone in stitches with the judge spluttering 'Not guilty' at the end of the proceedings. What happens is a bit of grovelling and an inane and insincere apology followed by several stiff drinks in the nearest pub. Not the happy hour, but the remorse hour.

Just before I went into hospital – and this is a sordid story that warrants no detail – I collected a criminal record for kicking someone's car parked annoyingly on the pavement. A CID plain-clothes man arrested me in the Coach on a charge of criminal damage and took me to Vine Street where I was fingerprinted and photographed. But this is extraordinary. As we walked past the Swiss pub on our way to the nick the arresting detective said, 'You screwed the landlord's daughter here in 1976, didn't you?' Well, I was amazed. How anyone could have known what went on that

Terry Jones, Jeremy Madden-Simpson, myself and Conan Nicholas of cat-racing fame.

Christmas Day after lunch on the saloon bar floor after the guvnor went upstairs for a nap I'll never know. But I liked the magistrate at Bow Street when I went up for the car kicking. He looked at my record and saw I'd been nicked last October for going over the top in the Raj of India restaurant and said, 'The last time it was rubber plants, Mr Bernard. Now it's cars. What next?' Well, you tell me, I thought. Probably a collector of taxes, possibly a drama student, maybe a black bird with the treble up of thrush, herpes and AIDS. All I know is that when I leave this flat it gets bloody dangerous. No wonder vultures are nesting on the roof of the Coach and Horses.

Bygones

Many years ago, round about 1950, I sparred three rounds one morning in Jack Solomon's gymnasium with Al Phillips, The Aldgate Tiger, when he was European and Empire featherweight champion. He knocked seven kinds of shit out of me and then patted me on my numbed head and said, 'Don't step out of your class, son.' Why on earth I should remember that last week as I came off the wagon and opened a bottle of Schadenfreude 1976, heaven alone knows. Until that moment of weakness, when I stretched out my hand for the corkscrew, I'd been reflecting on the sad business of Derek Jameson losing his libel battle against the BBC and about £75,000 into the bargain. Now, I must point out to you that I've never been one to bear grudges. I can barely remember the last time someone did me down and while it's true that Mr Jameson sacked me from the *Daily Express* when he took over in 1976 and sent me sprawling back into the gutter so to speak, I derive no satisfaction from his courtoom demise. Far from it. I take my hat off to any man with his background who can drag himself up by his own bootlaces, overcome almost every hurdle put in his way by a vindictive Mother Nature, and become editor of a national newspaper. It's true that when he did give me the tintack he did it in a very brusque – almost rude – way, but I'm sure that's just his manner and is the result of his retiring and shy way. An endearing disguise you might call it for a man bewildered at having so much so soon. But to reach for the stars and actually get the *Star* is something that goes to no man undeserved. After all, you only get out of life what you put into it.

What's awful is that I've also remembered I owe Mr Jameson an apology. He sat next to me and opposite Germaine Greer at a *Private Eye* lunch one day and Germaine and I were thoughtless enough to embark on a long and detailed discussion about oral sex. A pretty tactless thing to talk about in front of a man with working-class origins when you consider that oral sex is only indulged in by the middle and upper classes and therefore regarded as something of a treat by the workers. The good news is that Mr Jameson says he's actually got the £75,000. Paying it out is going to leave him pretty short but having it at all just goes to prove once again that the wiseacre who coined the phrase 'You only get out of life what you put into it' ranks with Edison, Marconi and Bell as a man who knew how to put it across. But you can't keep a good man down and I'm sure Mr Jameson will land on his feet, as he deserves to.

Life is far too short to bear malice, I always say. You play the cards you're dealt, as I did once with Richard Harris at Shepperton Studios. The fact that I lost every penny I had – he wouldn't play house rules – and that he wouldn't even give me the fare home matters not a fig and is now so blurred in my memory it is hardly worth mentioning.

But to go back to Mr Jameson for a minute before he recedes completely in my mind, what is worthy about him is the fact that he brought his action against the BBC on behalf of Fleet Street and not for his own gain. You've got to hand it to a man whose motives stem from a heart in the right place. Take Colin, one of my oldest friends. Years ago, I came to London for a weekend from Suffolk and had a sudden two-day affair with a girl friend of some long standing. Colin immediately telephoned my wife and told her, 'I think you ought to know, Jeff's been going to be bed with Helen.' 'Why are you telling me this, Colin?' asked my wife. 'Because I consider it my duty as a friend,' he said. There again I was in an awkward situation as I was later to be when Mr Jameson gave me the old heave-ho, but it hardly ever crosses my mind nowadays and I can't think why I should suddenly remember it. Anyway Colin asked me to lend him £50 the other day. It's a funny old life, isn't it?

Incidentally, I believe it was the man who said that you only get out of life what you put into it who also coined the phrase 'Let bygones be bygones' and I go along with that. I mean if I were to meet the sergeant who hit me over the head with a shovel when I was banged up in the guardhouse at Catterick in 1951 I'm sure we'd have a drink and a chat about old times. 'Hello, sarge. What are you having?' I'd say, trying to place his face. No, it would be an awful world if we couldn't forget and forgive. The Count of Monte Cristo and Dr Grimesby Roylott give me a pain. Do you remember when Roylott tells Sherlock Holmes, 'I am a dangerous man to fall foul of!' Revenge and threats – such a waste of time and energy. Anyway, good luck to what's his name. Oh yes, Jameson. I'd nearly forgotten.

Wrong track

This was in the *Sporting Life* of all papers last Friday: 'Three hundred youngsters commit suicide every year – many of them out of shame because they are not getting any sexual experiences, the Samaritans reported yesterday.' It made me wonder if the Samaritans have any figures for the amount of middle-aged people who are contemplating suicide out of shame because they are having too many sexual experiences with the *wrong* people. It also made me wonder just who the hell are the *right* people. As for the aforementioned youngsters I didn't give them much thought, although it must be a sad business for their friends and relatives. After all, although I can remember long and fairly painful bouts of celibacy at around the age of 18, when girls only fancied you if you were about 40, like being broke it's no reason – or a very bad one – for killing yourself. Admittedly I did have a flash of melancholy at Cheltenham on Gold Cup day when a girl in one of the bars told me that she could just about fancy me if I was 20 years younger but it passed with the arrival of the next round. Yes, I thought 20 years a bit cruel but then it's always some consolation, if you need it, to look at the young twerps who are 20 years and more younger under whom these girls bestow their favours. And is it in fact a favour?

Anyway, at the time of reading that small but sad news item, I was travelling on the Orient Express to Cheltenham sipping champagne, and that's not a situation conducive to considering suicide or the young or both. The Pullman car I was travelling in, 'Cygnus', had been part of Churchill's funeral train in 1965. What a way to go. The free champagne was rather good but how come it's called free when the day return comes to £140? They served canapes on the way down and a three-course dinner on the way back the main course of which was cold on a very cold day. Steak and kidney pudding would have been more in order but who can complain when the ticket is a kind and generous present?

By Paddington my train of thought had me contemplating those suicidal youngsters again and wondering just how many of them would complain if they did have those sexual experiences they were

158

ashamed of missing. How long would they have had to postpone their suicides to discover that we're most of us rather disappointing to each other? Of course, it's no good trying to tell them that a dog can be disappointed in 'his day' and it would be completely pointless to try to explain to them the enormous sense of relief I felt last week when I decided to close down the Great Portland Street Academy for Young Women and cancel our Summer School. The trouble is that the three hundred who ride annually into the valley of shame just don't know what they're missing and what you're missing isn't always altogether a good thing. Reading yet another boring piece about the menopause, this time in last Sunday's *Observer*, I looked at the four photographs of women supposedly suffering or about to suffer that state and to think that they could have male teenagers reaching for the barbiturates and gas taps was and is truly depressing. There are more career-minded, fitness-freaked, liberal ladies like Jane Fonda in Fleet Street than you can shake a stick at. Every trattoria in London has a Joan Collins in it. I cringe to think that's what I wanted when I was what the Samaritans call a 'youngster'.

What I fear I have missed is a sexual experience with the manageress of my local launderette. She's as solid as the figurehead of a tea clipper. She has a nicotine stain which runs from her upper lip to the bridge of her nose from the permanent fag stuck in her foul mouth. She coughs so you can hear her coming. She doesn't bother with make-up like Joan Collins. She's gone to seed completely and finds it cosy. She'd like to shoot those who don't 'fit in'. She's bad tempered, she sulks and she's lazy. She sometimes mentions her husband and her lip curls at the thought of him. She even sneers at my best shirts, shakes her head and taps her foot at my approach. In short, she is devoid of any sort of nonsense. She could make lemmings turn back. At the sight of her, suicidally inclined youngsters would split the heavens with a rendering of 'Jerusalem'. She may be the woman I've been looking for for years, and all the time I thought it was Veronica Lake, Anne Sheridan and Ava Gardner.

Back-scratching

Up until this week the large vodkas in Wiltshire have been as few and far between as Bernard Levin's full stops. Only the most appalling withdrawal symptons have forced me to turn over an old leaf, but at least I'm sleeping again at night. Could you believe an itch so bad as to drive you almost to tears? I had it once before in the Middlesex Hospital when the nurses bathed me from head to foot in Calamine lotion and then, when that didn't work, held me under too hot and too cold showers. That didn't do a lot either and eventually they filled me up with tranquillisers. You'd think that these people would carry vodka for medicinal purposes, which is just what I've now had to resort to although I'm a gregarious drinker. Speaking of which, the Flat Racing season is with us again thank God and I've never seen as many people fall off the wagon as they did last Saturday in the Members' Enclosure at Salisbury. It's good to see the old faces again and it's amazing how well they wear considering the battering they get from April till November. Apart from the activity in the Members' Bar it was backing my first loser of the season that stopped my back itching. By the third race it had sweat running down it, but the afternoon ended well enough when my man in Crompton, Gavin Hunter, tipped me his 7-1 winner. But Salisbury Racecourse is to be recommended anyway, being as it is a damned sight more friendly and attractive than a London betting shop. Now, it really is high time they did something to tart up betting shops. With three million people out of work you couldn't really say that a comfortable shop would discourage the workers from going about their business. What you should be able to get in the ideal betting shop, apart from a nasty fright, is a drink, a snack, a cheque cashed, every single race televised on a new channel and a free taxi ride home if you lose.

But, as I say, civilised racing is back with us until November and don't the most extraordinary things progress from that contest at 2 p.m.? After Salisbury last Saturday, I went to Lambourn for a splendid dinner and then finally put paid to the dreadful back itch with several Sunday lunchtime cocktails in the Swan at Great Shelford. Nothing to it really. A jolly nice day with lunch at the

With *Private Eye* as Colonel Mad, with Martin Tompkinson and editor
Richard Ingrams.

Lords, with the *Sunday Express* literary editor, and then home on the
rattler sharing a carriage with a *Spare Rib* reader who threatened me
with violence. God knows what I've written to offend her, and God
only knows how she recognised me. Anyway – and this is what is
meant by strange things happening as the result of a day at the races
– I woke up the following morning wearing a pair of ladies' knickers.
Any transvestite tendencies I may have unconsciously harboured
over the years have been well suppressed and I really can't think how
this could have happened. As I have already reported, to the *Sporting
Life*, the removal of ladies' knickers in the Lambourn area has to be
power-assisted, and where it doesn't have to be power-assisted it's no

surprise and nothing to be grateful for. Nevertheless I awoke in the old Great Portland Street Academy for Young Ladies on Monday morning, beheld myself in the mirror, and thought I was looking fairly attractive. But before I asked myself out for lunch I suddenly saw who I was. (And she wasn't going to pay the bill.)

I fear it's going to continue in a like vein for quite a while. We have Newbury this weekend and the promised appearance of El Gran Senor. The owner, Robert Sangster, one of the few men I've ever met with money who is not as tight as a drum, I'd like to see win although he doesn't actually need the prize money. It's his trainer, Vincent O'Brien, who bugs me a little. A man who was too nervous to talk to Colonel Mad in the old days is simply too nervous for anything. And, talking of not winning medals, Dave, the guvnor of the *Spectator* pub, the Duke of York, tells me that new *Spectator* employees have been seen buying their *own* drinks with money plucked from *purses*. This is rock bottom and such men should be shot or working for the *Sun* where I'm told they're paid by the purseful. At least you don't meet them at the races during the balmy months.

Rambling

The Easter weekend in Wiltshire was rather special. It was warm and sunny enough to have tea in the garden every morning shortly after 9 a.m. and only Eve and the serpent were missing. Healthy-looking rabbits played in the field beyond the apple tree, cock pheasants strutted along the top of an old kitchen garden wall looking like part of a Chinese print, and two beehives I'd thought extinct erupted lazily all day long. There was a sweet smell from the bonfire I'd made of dead ivy and brambles, and jays and magpies fought over some old bread I'd put out on a tree stump. In the afternoons I sat there with my long, iced drink feeling like a pissed badger who'd gatecrashed a Beatrix Potter party. But it was quite beautiful. I could almost hear everything growing. That, of course, is nonsense. I'm getting carried away. I could hear sweet fuck all and to rectify the situation I went inside and put on *Le Sacre du Printemps* so that I could hear it through the window. It seemed appropriate and

I'd been thinking of Miss Rite, as usual, anyway. Then I remembered with some irritation a remark of Stravinsky's that he made some time ago to the effect that there should be no such things as gramophone records and that people should listen only to live performances of music. He should have been locked up in a bedsitter or sat down in a garden 70 miles from the Festival Hall for a few months.

Another source of irritation was and is the love affair Radio 3 are having with Richard Strauss. To escape from him later I switched over to Radio 4 and bumped into *Desert Island Discs*. The guest was Lucy something, the woman who'd intentionally stranded herself on a tropical island with a man she'd had to marry for the purpose. At one point Roy Plomley asked her what she was doing now – now that she'd finished her book about the experience. She said – with a show-jumping accent – that she'd got 'the writing-bug'. I couldn't believe my ears. The *writing bug*? I waited with bated vodka for her to tell us where and how she'd got it, but she was far too crafty for that. It's certainly just about the only virus that's eluded me, but give the Lucys of this world a pen and paper and they're infected immediately. (I remember when John Pilger first caught the writing bug. Years ago he reported from Little Rock that 'night came down like a red velvet curtain'. I'd like to know what he'd been drinking.)

Anyway, I can't get Lucy out of my mind. Not only did she get stranded on her sandy strip without the help of an Arts Council grant, but she says she stopped having sex with her old man shortly after they hit the beach. First, I think that all right-minded people will join with me in proposing that the Arts Council commission a ship on the Greenpeace type of line for writers who want to write books about being stranded on desert islands. Secondly, I think we should be told what her husband did for sex after the nights started coming down. I have managed without sex since I got stranded in Wiltshire on Good Friday, but I do have television.

And now, as I sit listening to my first cuckoo in my little Eden awaiting a long overdue invitation from Roy Plomley to go on his programme, I wonder more about his last two questions – what luxury would you take and what two books apart from the Bible and Shakespeare? – than I do about the music. What people choose for their luxury on *Desert Island Discs* has often puzzled me. Champagne, for example, is surely an essential and not a luxury. Marie Antoinette wasn't uncaring, she simply had her priorities right – although she did in fact suggest croissant not cake. I suppose a telephone is useless enough to be considered a luxury but I think I'd have to choose a large supply of morphine. As for the Bible or Shakespeare they're the last two books I'd take. I find the Bible is one of the most depressing books I've come across and there are far too many words and phrases in Shakespeare that I don't understand. It's a toss up between *The Wind in the Willows, The Complete Sherlock Holmes* and *The Count of Monte Cristo. Monte Cristo* is the greatest of plots and revenge is indeed sweet. *Treasure Island* runs it close but the good guys are a bit wet and I could only like Jim Hawkins if I thought he went into a rapid decline after cashing in his loot or went in search of Long John Silver. And was the *Hispaniola* fitted out with the aid of an Arts Council grant? Such imponderables afflict me in the solitude of this garden. It is time to return to the reality of the Coach & Horses.

Game try

I think I very nearly died last Sunday. I was sitting in the garden watching the filthy pheasants mating – they really ought to call it a day now that it's May – and I suddenly was sick and had the most awful pain in my chest. It was probably heart attack number one. Minutes after that a bee-keeper arrived to add some boxes to the hives outside to extend them and make room for more honey. I happen to be frightened of most things that sting, apart from women and editors, and when I told the bee-keeper so he said to stay well clear of the hives during thundery weather. It puts them in something of a tizz. Anyway, all that didn't do much to improve the pain in the chest.

No sooner had the bee-keeper gone than a young woman knocked on the door and asked me, 'Are you the gamekeeper?' Now do I look like a gamekeeper, I ask you? Is a gamekeeper to be found in a garden at 11 a.m. nursing a heart and a large vodka? And does a gamekeeper wear jeans and a blazer? But she looked rather nourishing so I asked her in and implied that although I was not a gamekeeper I was willing to learn and had in the past four weeks introduced many pheasants to each other. But she wasn't in the mood for playing, so I went back into the garden to soak up some

My two lovely personal agony aunts, Sally Vincent and Irma Kurtz.

more sun and more elevenses. Then I saw an extraordinary thing. A rabbit and a weasel having a fight. The weasal won inside the distance, biting the rabbit in the neck. I don't trust a rabbit that I haven't killed myself, so I didn't stew it and threw it over the fence into the field. Within five minutes it was being pecked by rooks.

Mother Nature is working overtime in Wiltshire and she's taken a job in your actual Salisbury itself. When I went into the New Inn on Friday just for the one between Marks & Spencer and the delicatessen, who should walk in but a load of old Fleet Street faces. Now, as it happens, I'm not crazy about journalists, but it was delightful to see the likes of Paul Curran, John Akass and Ed Vine. It was the first time I've seen men in Salisbury who didn't flinch in front of the bar. And why should they? It was estimated in the Coach & Horses last Monday that John Pilger earns something in the region of £40,000 a year, which is enough for a round of drinks. Anyway, the aforementioned hacks brought a tone of civility to a pub where a man had been talking to me for thirty minutes about the weather.

What is vitally important about the weather is the dependency on it of the state of the going. Saturday sees the 2,000 Guineas and any drops of rain between now (Tuesday) and then will lessen the chances of Keen which I've had the biggest bet on that I've struck for years. That in itself should stop it from winning, but I can't forget the way Lester was looking nonchalantly over his shoulder for non-existent dangers fully a furlong from home when he won last time. When Lester does that it's something akin to seeing Ian Botham walk down the wicket before the ball has left the bowler's arm. To give you a further warning I have inflicted a penalty on the French filly L'Orangerie for the 1,000 Guineas. But a friend of mine who owns a few garages tells me that he's had £8,000 to £15,000 on El Gran Senor for the 2,000 Guineas. I think it's quite crazy since I don't think that 15-8 is particularly good value in a Classic race. What's more he's had £2,000 to win on Mahogany for the 1,000 Guineas. Both horses are considered to be unbeatable by their stables, and so was Sonny Liston when the then Cassius Clay dumped him on his arse at 8-1.

But I do think that there should be Arts Council grants for those of us punters who need a bottle of Dutch courage before they can write out a cheque for more than they can afford to put on a horse. In the unlikely event of Keen winning – God knows the owner, Lord Howard de Walden, needs the prize money – this column should be datelined Istanbul next week. Maybe Bombay, since they're still racing there. But, come what may, I shall be at Epsom on 6 June to see Rainbow Quest win the Derby, and then probably Barbados after Siberian Express has won at Ascot. If all fails I suppose I could get a job as a gamekeeper since I appear to look the part.

Ups and downs

Out of doors it has been a somewhat high life recently, and here in my flat it has been very low indeed. Last Saturday at Newmarket, 2,000 Guineas day, I was rubbing shoulders with millionaires and Charles Benson at a superb pre-race and buffet lunch and the day before in London I had lunch with Alice Thomas Ellis. The latter occasion was a slice of high life that not even Taki would aspire to. But in the early morning, and as soon as the sun has gone down, it has been very low indeed. I see the signs of a nasty descent. When you aim a dirty tissue at a waste-paper basket and it misses and you can't be bothered to pick it up, look out. When you go two days without shaving, feel too lazy to wash up, water the plants, empty the ashtrays, go to the launderette, iron a shirt or pay the milkman and just lie there on your bed nursing a stomach slightly distended with gastritis and wondering just why it is that the world does *not* owe you a living, a good woman, the urge to work and a less haunted face then it's time to pull yourself together, if you happen to have the blueprint for 'together'.

Now why is it that people like Robert Sangster never miss the waste-paper basket? Possibly because they haven't got anything to throw away. And, Charles St George's Newmarket lunch apart, I have to own up to sinking so low as to have lived on frozen food for the past two days. A Birds Eye cod steak in mushroom sauce doesn't exactly inspire one to rape a typewriter and on the Bank Holiday Monday I watched no less than four consecutive films on television. I'd very much like to reverse the location and time of day of these highs and lows. I feel I ought to spring-clean, empty the dustbins, spend a bomb at Sketchley's, pluck up the courage to see what or who is under the bed and attend to them, and then, and only then, go out for lunch at Claridges and fall asleep with my face in the soup, burn holes in the tablecloth and reveal the holes in my socks as the waiters eject me. Those of you who aren't addicted to extreme positions or situations probably don't understand, and good for you. Stay in your happy medium as long as you can.

The late lamented painter Robert McBryde summed it up. I saw him one morning actually ironing a shirt with a table-spoon he kept holding over a gas-stove flame. He was a real stickler. Then, of course, he'd go out and by evening most likely he would have spewed up a litre of wine over that shirt. I suppose the secret of a well-kept, orderly life is to care *all* the time. McBryde was awfully good in the morning. I was very good all the time on the wagon between 1972 and 1975, even taking books off the shelf to dust them, would you believe. In fact I became so caring that it was only a sudden bottle of whisky that stopped me blowing my brains out. (And please don't tell me I would have to be a sniper to do that.)

But talking vaguely of a sort of squalor, I made a fairly rare visit to

167

the old Colony Room Club the other day to meet Cosmo Landesman who interviewed me for *Time Out*. I fear I gave too much away and if you're listening out there, Cosmo, please don't be too unkind. On second thoughts, sex, alcohol and horseracing haven't really destroyed me, they've simply impeded the progress to Haslemere where, as some readers may remember, I always intended to settle down with a wife, two children – one of each sort, of course – a lawn mower, Ford Escort and steady job. Let's drop it unless you really need the money. Anyway, I stand for everything *Time Out* readers despise. Instead, since you're not a man of extremes, why don't you write to our editor here and suggest a column in between Taki and me? You could call it 'Still life'.

Quails' eggs

Remaining and regular readers may remember that some time ago I mentioned the strange case of the Coutts Bank doorman whom I came across one morning when I entered the Strand branch some years ago on a begging mission. The fact that I had an account there was in no way flash. It was simply that IPC banked there and I was working at the time for the *Daily Mirror*. Anyway, I walked in one morning only to find the commissionaire doing the *Times* crossword puzzle. This was something of a psychological setback. I recorded the fact in the back of my mind but never mentioned it again until recently when I paid a call to the Chelsea Arts Club to find the doorman reading Henry James. That provoked a tiny correspondence and again put me in my place. Until then and this last week I'd always felt it slightly comforting to spend the time of day with my inferiors, since doing so always makes it so easy to be nice, but last week I got the literary soporific punch – as Gene Tunney called his when he whacked Hemingway for showing off – when I walked into Maxim's in Panton Street to find a remarkable doorman called Duncan reading no less a student of form than Nietzsche.

Now, as you may recall my telling you, I once got duffed up by a fellow coal miner in Hanley Deep pit in 1953 for taking my lunch (snapping) down the pit wrapped up in the *Times*, but never did I read Proust in my dressing-room before a fight in my boxing days and

With Robert Sangster at Goodwood.

never did I get discovered reading Sir Thomas Browne between dishes when I was washing up in Lyons Corner House in Tottenham Court Road many years ago. I have to admit to a mild flirtation with Byron on a building site, but Nietzsche in a cloakroom takes the biscuit.

But, anyway, Maxim's I can recommend. I kicked off with poached haddock garnished with quails' eggs, followed on with roast duck and red beans, and finished with a fruit salad that comprised West Indian and oriental fruits. It is a nicely done up restaurant – art nouveau – and my companion, unlike the food writer's companion, picked up the bill which I had the good manners not to look at and which came to £35. On the way out I had a word with Duncan the doorman – I made a somewhat jocular remark about Nietzsche – and he told me that he usually reads his books in the original German. He further informed me that he knew who I was and that he has a subscription to the *Spectator*. I have seen a buffet car attendant on a train reading *New Society* and I have seen a derelict on a park bench using the *New Statesman* as a napkin but I doubt very much whether these people had your actual subscription. I can only surmise that there must be money in being a doorman and that the plunge from navvying into journalism was a grave error on my part.

Anyway, after Maxim's the day deteriorated. I went to the Coach & Horses and had a few drinks with my friend Graham Mason. After what we in the business call 'the one', Graham suddenly assaulted my right knuckle with his face and I am writing to you with great difficulty at this moment since my fourth and fifth metacarpals were then broken by his belligerent forehead. The hand that once attempted an ineffectual tattoo on Sandy Saddler's face when he was featherweight champion of the world is now out of action. And this is not the first time Graham has hurt me. He once refused to give me our mutual doctor's telephone number when I'd run out of insulin in the Swiss Tavern and he once turned off my drip when he came to visit me in hospital. Could he be trying to give me some sort of hint? The broken hand does of course mean that I can't write out a cheque to William Hill for the money their man on the rails lent me at Newmarket and if this typewriter wasn't electric I'd be in the Coach drinking with my left hand. I shall have to learn to kick like Taki. And the awful 'High life' man has had me thrown out of his cottage, which has screwed up the forthcoming summer. His facetious remarks concerning my having left enough vodka on the premises to keep a Cossack regiment happy were taken at face value by his landlady and she now considers me to be undesirable. A platoon or troop possibly, but not a regiment; certainly not a doorman.

Jeremy

Yet another friend has died and I feel as much angry as sad at what seems like a monstrous injustice. Jeremy Madden-Simpson – christened by Eva whose obituary I had to write here eighteen months ago as Jeremy Madman-Simpleton – was a dear friend and Irish nutter who hadn't long turned 40. To see him in the Coach & Horses flailing his arms around like a windmill while still managing to cling on to a pint of cider, it probably wouldn't have occurred to you that he'd been taught history by Cardinal Home at Ampleforth. When I was on the brink last year in St Stephen's Hospital he used to visit me every evening and bring me a croissant for my breakfast the next day and when a piss artist takes time off during licensed hours to visit you then you know you've got a real friend. I teased him a few times in this column about his being barred from the Queen's Elm for an age but he was happily reinstated a few weeks ago. You wouldn't want to see a man die while he was barred from a pub.

But it wasn't all pubs and wine bars with us. In the summer – and we were planning to start again next week – we used to go to the ice-cream parlour at Harrods in the morning before opening time and giggle over strawberry milkshakes. Then, sometimes, we'd have breakfast in Fortnum and Mason. We first got really friendly after I broke a bone in my right hand on him one night in the French pub and he'd often laugh at the fact that neither of us could remember why, and he'd say, 'What on earth was *that* about?', and then add 'Well, if you can't hit a friend, who can you hit?' What's rotten is that he'd recently found a good woman and was very happy, and God's timing stinks. And why aren't the real shits dead and why do the people who've been given warnings survive? Of course, a lot of grieving isn't only grief for oneself but sheer selfishness. Frank Norman, Eva, Bryce and now Jeremy won't be walking into the Coach today, actually *pleased* to see you and showing it, and it's so bloody inconsiderate of them.

Needless to say, one thinks of one's own death constantly, and sharp, painful reminders such as friends' deaths make me wonder whether this interval on earth might be nonsense in spite of the past good days and times. The lunchtime sessions in the Coach with Jeremy and Tom Baker and Conan Nicholas were worth all the trappings of all the success stories you've ever heard and I'd rather keep down with the likes of Jeremy than keep up with the awful Joneses. Anyway, I had something of a whip-round to get some flowers for his funeral last night and contributions came from a club owner, three pornographers, an editor, a barrow boy, a shipping clerk and a publican, and in the space of fifteen minutes. He would have liked the assortment. And shuffling off this mortal coil I look around at or think of friends and it seems as though we're in a queue that's shuffling along towards a sort of bus stop. 'Who's next?' 'No, sorry. You were before me.'

There's a dreadful fellow in the French pub who once tried to make a 'book' on who in Soho was next for the long jump. I'm told he made me 5-4 favourite for the event but the long shots keep going in and, although I'm pleased to survive, it's a lousy race to have been entered for. So now, of course, as self-obsessed as the next man, Jeremy's death makes me dwell on my own wretched mortality and another birthday tomorrow compounds the morbidity. My ex-wife observed that all I thought about was myself, and she may have been very nearly right, but right now I wish to God that I believed in God. The party could go on. Different premises but no closing time. Possibly like a sterilised Colony Room Club. I wish now that I'd never snapped at Jeremy and told him to pull himself together. Thankfully he ignored the order. The trouble is that there aren't that many people about who are instant laughter, and I fear we're running out of heads to break knuckles on. He deserved better than that. I should have hit him over the head with a bottle of champagne and launched him into something much better. Fucking hell, that reminds me, he owes me a fiver.

Party spirit

The past few days have been a bit of a thrash and it's got to stop. Starting tomorrow it's all going to be different. But my birthday party and my friends thereat quite overwhelmed me last weekend and I'm finding it hard to settle down again to the smooth, quiet old routine of screaming at Norman and writing my pieces in the betting shop. The weekend began badly though. My broken hand started to swell up, alarmingly for a man with sugar in his bloodstream, so I took it up to the Middlesex Hospital at closing time, where I was quite unnecessarily and childishly rude to a charming nurse in casualty called Sheila. Half an hour later I went back and apologised to her and then said: 'You must get some horrible people in here on Saturday nights; much worse than me.' She said, 'No. Not worse. In fact you're the worst I've seen for weeks.' I find that pretty hard to believe, but it could confirm my guess that being drunk is being temporarily insane. (So is falling in love, but that's another story and not a very nice one.)

But all was well the next day, I assaulted Del Monico with a cheque and dear Norman added to the booty by giving me a present of a bottle of Smirnoff – why don't these people get their own bloody PR? – and the party began before moving off to a friend's flat for the party proper. Being a geriatric suddenly didn't seem too bad at all. Friends brought presents into the Coach – books mostly – and it was all very moving. Irma Kurtz gave me something rather unusual, a gold-and-enamel money clip consisting of the seal of the President of the United States and engraved with the signature of the contemptible Richard Nixon.

And, speaking of Nixon, a lady friend taped the talks during the session in the Coach. I played it back again today, and it really is quite extraordinary to hear the nonsense most of us utter when we're holding a glass. The subject of sex cropped up immediately, of course, and one group of us were going on about just what turned us on. One woman actually said she was once excited by a man carrying some fenugreek seeds about his person. Very odd, and it reminded me of the night years ago in the Pickwick Club when someone poured an entire jugful of sauce tartare into my jacket pocket because they thought it was a good idea at the time. But I must try fenugreek, although I should have thought that money would be more sexually exciting to most women. And speaking of sauces I woke up the other morning and found my left shoe half full of the Bolognese variety. It makes you wonder what on earth happens in the middle of the night.

Anyway, the party went very well. No one hit anyone and, if they had done, it wouldn't have mattered much anyway since both Doctors Finlay and Who were in attendance. Old fans of *Dr Finlay*'s *Casebook* would have been stunned and delighted to see him dance a few Highland reels. My chicken cooked in tarragon and anointed with lemon and cream sauce went down pretty well and the drink actually held out. The next morning I was served beautifully cold bubbly in a bubble bath. I strongly recommend champagne in the bath as a way to start the day, but you can find your own waitress. The contrast between the temperatures of the bird, bath and champagne can be very invigorating and, as Norman said, I've had the punishment, now I want the nourishment. Bubbles apart, I can also recommend drinking very cold dry Martinis in a very hot bath as a way of proceeding through the afternoon towards dinner.

Well, anyway, the party's over and we now have to tread rather gingerly through another year. Epsom beckons on Wednesday and it just might be a very good Derby indeed. I can't back odds-on favourites, so El Gran Senor won't have the added burden of my money. Norman, as usual, will get that.

Snapdragon

I was delighted last Sunday to read about the New York woman who pumped five bullets into her husband. He got a divorce on the grounds that she was 'unsafe to live with'. Bliss. How much better than the usual slow poison of marriage. I read about it on a buffetless train to Basingstoke and reflected that I should, by rights and on the law of averages, contain no less than twenty bullets. Anyway, you don't go to Basingstoke for fun, and I went there to get to Kingsclere where two good friends of mine barbecued two-and-a-half lambs. Gaston Berlemont, *le patron* of the French pub, carved the beasts, and at 3.30 p.m. I watched my £25 on Darshaan romp home in the Prix du Jockey Club – French Derby to you – at 3-1 and had a splendid day. Or did I? You see, the thing is or was, I met no less than six ex-ladies, and it breaks my bloody heart to think about what was, could have been and might have been. I felt particularly sad to meet again the lovely woman whose parting words to me years ago were 'You've snapped at me for the last time'. It was an extremely unpleasant way to get fired, and I wish she'd pumped five bullets into me instead.

Anyway, the faces from the past filled me with an awful feeling of regret, and sadness has descended on Great Portland Street this morning like some great awful wet blanket, although I shall cross the street shortly to collect £75 from my beloved bookmaker Victor Chandler. It isn't my ambition to get in Pseuds Corner again, but it has to be thought, if not written, that we're pretty awful to each other on occasion, and it's a shame. And shame is the word. What's worse is that none of us have snapped at each other for the last time and we shall go on snapping like dragons until we drop.

Apart from ex-girlfriends, there were some old men-friends I hadn't seen for years, and one of them made me squirm with that sort of patronising attitude they have when they think they've left you for dead in the rat race.

As I say, the afternoon was akin to stirring up the mud from the bottom of a clear pond. Perhaps worse than 'You've snapped at me for the last time' are the faces you've simply drifted away from. 'You

174

don't bring me flowers any more' is one of my favourite songs, but it reminds me of 'You don't fucking telephone me any more', which is my most unfavourite unwritten song. The recriminations in the eyes are horrible reminders of things past. Faces shuffle with embarrassment. Past intimacies gather in the mind and you suddenly remember that we go on and on *hurting* each other. I do anyway. Francis Bacon keeps telling me that the only way to get through the business of life is to regard almost everything as being utterly unimportant, but looking at those old faces makes it hard to do. This is a squalid little mini-tragedy, and I think that's about enough self-pity for one week.

The day ended cheerfully enough in the bar on Waterloo Station of all places. If Victor Chandler had offered 25-1 against me drinking in Waterloo Station with four women and two men while discussing sex on a Sunday evening at eight o'clock I wouldn't have taken it. But there it is. What an amazing jemmy to the door of the mind is a few large vodkas. Smirnoff 6 Mesmer 0. Then from Waterloo to the Coach, and yet another old flame was rekindled. Thomas Hardy put it best. 'These market dames, mid-aged, with lips thin drawn and tissues sere – are they the ones we loved years agone and courted here?' Enough of that. I write to you on Derby day and not much else matters at the moment. Win or lose I'm off to Chantilly on Saturday for the Prix de Diane, the French Oaks, run on Sunday. It's a pretty little town with no old flames to bring me down.

Big noise

I keep meeting women, employed either by Lord Matthews or Rupert Murdoch, who think that because they can type they can therefore write. Normally, I don't bump into these creatures, but recently I've been having to pop in and out of Fleet Street since bread needs butter. And what a ghastly place it is. The pubs are the pits, and the restaurants are rather shabby. Worse, and worst, is the conversation in the pubs, if you can call talking incessant shop conversation. Journalism is a function, like going to the lavatory, best done at home and not talked about. Last week I took my little niece to see an editor in an attempt to get her lift-off in Fleet Street. The next thing

I'll know is that she'll be drinking large gins and tonic and wearing her sunglasses on top of her head – a disgusting female habit, being, I suppose, the female equivalent of macho. Could there be a word for it? Facho? Whatever it is, Germaine Greer has bundles of it. As is a red rag to a bull, a chocolate éclair to Bernard Levin or a sheet of typing paper to an office girl in Fleet Street, so a television camera has become to Ms Greer. Oh, how I envy people who like themselves. One could just sail through life.

It has always fascinated me to see and watch just what success, 'making' it and fame do to people. The effects can be extraordinary. With women, like Ms Greer, they just can't stop talking and they, of course, *always* know best. Men usually, and quite simply, become dreadfully self-important. Some of them, idiots, crack. A few years ago, I went on the piss with Mick Jagger and in a club called the Kismet, but known as the Iron Lung, he suddenly burst into tears. Solicitous as a spider to a fly, I enquired as to the cause of the dreadful stream of tears and mucus ruining my lapels. 'I can't take it,' he howled. 'What can't you take, you fat-lipped twit?' I asked him gently. 'The success. The money and all those birds.' At the time, I happened to be short of both requisites and suggested a transfer of both cash and crumpet into my safekeeping. He soon stopped crying and left without paying. My turn to cry. George Best went to pieces. I took him to lunch one day and he turned up with three girls. Three. I've done some strange things in my time but I've always found two to be quite ample. You can't get near Michael Parkinson any more, and Colin Welland, known to all and sundry in Gerry's Club as Smelly Welland, is damn-nigh certifiable.

But all this strange behaviour is the result of deep-seated fear, the cause of halitosis (or, to be more accurate, it's their friends who do the suffering). And I believe it to be fear that makes Ms Greer talk too much, and fear that has motivated her into acquiring more knowledge than you or I have on any subject in the conversational repertoire. ('Speak for yourself,' I hear Someone say.) She also needs to be told that an unhappy childhood is not a suitable topic for conversation. It is not unique. I too had no sticks to my lollipops and had to wet the bed standing on my head. An introductory chapter on an unhappy childhood is permissible in an autobiography, but you should never go on television and whine to the viewers that your mother in Wagga Wagga didn't have a reading-ticket to the London Library when you were five.

It may surprise you to know that I've had a little of all this

Enjoying a joke with Norman.

nonsense, albeit on a small circuit. In 1970, when I was the *Sporting Life* columnist, I was quite the little Jack the Lad on the racecourse. Strangers kept buying me drinks and I was pissed from Christmas to Marble Arch. But it didn't make my breath smell and I refrained from telling my hosts that my mother once clipped me over the ear for having a dip into her handbag while I thought her back was turned during an air raid. Anyway, at least my daughter thinks I'm famous still. I must be careful not to breathe all over her – just in case it's catching.

Dynamite

Last Saturday at Sandown Park I exceeded my humble expectations. The Eclipse Stakes, now the horribly named Coral Eclipse Stakes, is one of the best events in the calendar and I try not to miss it. The first man I met walking through the entrance was Robert Sangster, who is a delightful fellow in spite of having £100 million in his current account. (It's extraordinary to think that he wins the pools *every* week.) He told me that he and Vincent O'Brien strongly fancied Sadler's Wells, so I steamed in immediately and had £25 at 4-1. Not a lot, but quite a lot if that's all you're holding. Then I had a tenner on Grooming, which obliged at 3-1, and finally £50 on Special Vintage, which won at 5-2. For a moment I began to wonder whether maybe I'm not quite as daft as I know I am. I then had a quiet celebration in the bar, was driven back to London, had another private party, passed out in Someone's flat and woke up at midnight surrounded by a bevy of beauties. One particular beauty seemed strangely more interested in sitting on Somebody else's knee and climbing all over him than she did in your Low life correspondent. Perhaps the girl who told me last week, 'You're a mean, little, alcoholic, diabetic prick,' could have been near the mark.

Then Sunday was pretty awful. I read an obituary of Flora Robson in which she was quoted as having once said, 'I have had little personal love in my life.' What an awful thing to be able to say. I brooded about that over a cocktail or two, forgot that I'd been invited to lunch by my favourite author, Alice Thomas Ellis, and spent the evening kicking myself for my bad manners and embarrassing amnesia. (I've got a lunch today, but where and who with?)

Apart from Sandown Park, the other good thing was verification of another trip to Barbados in September without anyone from the *Sun, Honey,* the *Guardian* woman's page or *Spare Rib.* It has taken me two weeks to recover from the thirst in Norway inflicted on me by the impenetrable handbag of a Fleet Street colleague I mentioned last week. Should my man who has fixed this West Indian jaunt inform me at the last minute that we are, after all, to be accompanied by a similarly overpaid hackette carrying a replica of Fort Knox over her shoulder, I shall take a stick of dynamite with me.

When I think of these people it comes as no surprise to read that thirty per cent of 2,000 American women recently interviewed claimed that they would do 'better than average in a fist fight'. What happened to women? Where did it all go wrong? Again, like the decline in the quality of life, I think it must have started with rock and roll. By the time the Beatles were established and the Wolfenden Report had wrecked Soho and established the porn industry, all life was low unless you happened to be holding bread. In 1962 a woman ironed a shirt for me. She didn't engage me in a fist fight. She even went to bed with me, which is the next best thing.

Looking back on that sort of behaviour, I feel as though I'm peering at a distant Restoration comedy. I think they might well have been the good old days, although most of them were spent scratching around for the price of half a pint of bitter. I didn't get trips to Barbados, and the horses I backed ran rather slowly. I was once three months late with the rent of my Suffolk cottage, which was five shillings a week. But then I remember lying on the lawn in the garden of my pub in weather like this pretending to sleep but looking up the skirts of lady tourists and just listening to the bees buzz and the ice chink in the Pimms. Their Pimms. What days they could have been in Soho and Suffolk if I'd had my enormous wealth then.

Meanwhile it's Newmarket. The sales in the morning, lunch with Charles St George and then the races in the afternoon. Days like this can be dreadfully exhausting. It's all the standing. Just you try drinking champagne for eight hours on your feet with a snatched five minutes at the table for some fresh salmon. Well, it knocks me out anyway.

Fitted up

Last week in Salonika a soldier and a labourer were each sentenced to 14 years in jail for raping a 105-year-old woman. It reminded me of the Moroccan student I wrote about some time ago who raped a pelican and two German tourists on an Aegean island. Thank God we're saner in Britain. A friend tells me that a 76-year-old man in Aberdeen appeared in court charged with indecent behaviour with two schoolgirls. He was given a suspended sentence and the judge told him he wouldn't send him to prison seeing as how the girls assaulted *him* and that anyway it was his first offence. I personally wouldn't mind all that much if two schoolgirls sexually assaulted me, but I wouldn't like to have to wait until I was 76 for it to happen. The fact that it happened in Aberdeen makes me suspect that they were probably just trying to get some money out of his pocket.

The other news item I read was of the death of Jim Fixx, the man who started the jogging craze. I also note that Geoffrey Cannon, the eccentric who writes about health in the *Sunday Times* and who is jogging-mad, looks 76 although he is nearer 26. These people are courting disaster. They are also extremely narcissistic and if they choke on their bran and high fibre I don't give a fig. The only point in exercise and being fit is that it enables you to abuse yourself even more. Those people who live to tremendous ages in the Caucasus region thrive on sexual intercourse and vodka. Sex is better for the circulation than any exercise yet devised by man, and thanks to Smirnoff I have a very low cholesterol level. I can only conclude that if rabbits drank vodka they'd live to be 105 too. I suppose it's an inordinate fear of death that propels people into jogging on yoghurt-filled stomachs. We must all make way for the next generation, though. The alternative is unthinkable, unless you want to linger on and get raped by Greek soldiers or assaulted by Scottish schoolgirls.

What joggers and fibre-munchers should realise, though, is that gossip, and particularly malicious gossip, is one of the greatest progenitors of longevity. Name me a gossip who has been snatched away too soon. You can't. Benign people fade away, and joggers are benign. Put me on a desert island with a malignant. You can spot a malign unhealthy person from miles away. Like drunks, they have dodgy eyes. The whites are yellow going umber with red streaks. There's a nasty grin that plays around their wet lips when nothing whatsoever funny or amusing is being said. Their hands tremble and shake until they have plunged the metaphorical dagger between your shoulderblades. Then all is peace. They swill stories, expense lunches and unhappy memories. Above all, they understand the human condition, which is something the village idiot can't comprehend – and which is what makes him the villiage idiot. The village idiot is the man who mentally jogs through life. His is the mind made of the solid fibre and bran of the weather and the cost of bread and cheese. A *Sunday Times* health writer could never survive in such primitive and healthy conditions. There'd be nothing to investigate, no knocks.

Just for curiosity, I tried to do a few press-ups a few minutes ago. I couldn't manage one. Not one. I am also a failed arm wrestler. Neither of these short-comings prevents me from not dropping dead during a jog or a dig into the cornflakes bowl. I have had alarming moments of short breath in the peace of my bed and I can no longer sprint after buses. But I still prefer to keep my hair – how did you lose yours, Geoffrey Cannon? Bad diet? Lack of shampoo? – and, as long as I can raise my arm to hail a taxi, my right arm to sign a cheque and to raise a glass, and my right foot to trip up a jogger, I shall remain moderately contented with the body I live in. The trouble is that health freaks have made the holocaust an unlikely event. It will end up with a whimper. The human race will just jog and diet off the edge of this flat earth.

Nothing doing

My typewriter keeps giving me reproachful looks and obviously thinks I'm having an affair with a pub. What dear Monica Electric de Luxe can't comprehend is that it's she who's driving me to drink. She sits there on my desk buzzing with energy and simply aching to be touched, and all I can think about is how much I need a holiday. Now, you probably think, how the hell does he need a holiday since he does damn all anyway, but you do need to get away from nothing sometimes. Doing nothing is a drudge. Anyone can cover innocent pieces of paper with words, but doing nothing requires a mite of imagination. You don't really think I'm actually listening to those bores in the Coach & Horses, do you? Good God, no. I'm sitting there trying to conjure up dreams out of thick air.

Take this morning so far. It's been hell. I lay there in the bath a-while back, listening to a concerto for two pianos by Max Bruch. The announcer said the score had been lost, but some twit obviously found it and handed it into whatever you hand in lost scores to, which was a big mistake. After that, I lay on my bed and went through an instant replay of 1978. That wasn't very pretty and the script was awful, especially *her* lines. Then I burned my hand on the steam-iron and made a cup of tea, but the milk was sour. You're with me now. Beginning to get it? You see how much better it would have been this morning if I'd simply got up at 6 a.m. and raped Monica Olympia immediately. It's going to get worse, though. They don't open for another hour and a half. Then, when they do, I've got to do nothing until they close. I suppose someone will tell me how they spent the bank holiday. There will be the usual ribald remarks about the England cricket team being a load of wankers. Norman will tell someone to piss off, and his mother will give me the meteorological details of the situation in Harrow-on-the-Hill early this morning. Now, wouldn't you rather have a job than have to go through all this and that? Of course you would. I don't want to over-excite you, but after the Coach closes I have to go to the *Sporting Life* to write a column, the deadline for which is 5 p.m. when the White Hart opens, and in there I will have to listen to a lot of hacks telling me about the scoops they got years ago. After that I will probably have to go to a Greek kebab house in Charlotte Street where I will lose my reading glasses and then be asked to leave. And you think *you* need a holiday.

Even the forthcoming trip to Barbados in four weeks isn't going to be a holiday. First, I've got to keep a diary of it for a travel magazine, and secondly that means I've got to remember what I did the day before when I sit down to write the daily entry. And the party I'm going with is a very rich mixture. Apart from trying to make sure that Richard West doesn't drown (not an easy task for a non-swimmer), you should see the ladies we're with. Have you ever taken four Dobermanns for a walk? Don't. Yes, I've got to get away from it all. But what's on the other side of nothing? I'm seriously thinking of getting a job as a computer salesman or something of that kind. Ugh. The only thing that's keeping me going at the moment is the thought of filming *Opinions* for Channel 4 in a couple of weeks' time. The director already says – smirking at my script – that there will be a lot of complaints, so we will go out at 10 p.m. after the children have gone to bed. It is actually quite interesting and rather extraordinary how upset people can get over other people's life styles, and I wonder why. I think maybe they think your grass is greener than theirs, but heaven knows I'm living in a rubbish dump. I don't mean to offend Norman by saying that but let's face it, this isn't a formal garden at Blenheim – more a Dig for Victory allotment – we're in.

Which train of thought leads me to the war. I read a remarkable thing the other day in a book which is the history of the Prix de l'Arc de Triomphe. Apparently, when the war was declared, a steward of the Jockey Club said 'It is unthinkable that in a sporting country like England we should declare war before the St Leger.' Of course, the St Leger was called off – it's run at the end of September – but only an Englishman could say something like that. It's also rather overrating the Leger, even though it is a classic. And he had planned his holiday to coincide with the race, too. Well, my little holiday will coincide with the Arc in October and I shall be well pleased if Reagan can keep his finger off the button until they pass the post. With All Along passing it first, of course.

Nursing a hangover in Red Square.

Jaundiced

My body seems to have become more and more addicted to the Middlesex Hospital. Last Sunday I had to be admitted again to have a biopsy on a large lump which suddenly appeared in the mastoid region behind my left ear. From the post-operative pain I can only surmise that they have removed half my head, as opposed to taking a mere sample of it. It was the first time since my schooldays, which I can't anyway remember, that I'd had a general anaesthetic, and I don't like it. Added to which they gave me yet another local anaesthetic while I was out to the world. During the whole so-called trivial business I was also on an insulin drip, dextrose drip and a Hemanevrin drip. I had more tubes coming in and out of me than Piccadilly Circus. They seemed mildly surprised when, later, after a large injection of Valium as a bonus, I collapsed twice on their marble floor despoiling it with one of their school dinners. I feel sure that these things do not happen in the London Clinic.

But the day started badly enough and I was full of foreboding when, walking to the Middlesex, I found a dead cat in a plastic carrier bag on the doorstep of my local butcher's shop. It was a little sinister. Could it have been an inside job, or had some nasty person put it there as some sort of hint? Anyway, I arrived at the hospital and waited an interminable age to be seen by someone, and so was obliged to read the posh Sundays from cover to cover. You may imagine my horror when reading 'A Life in the Day of Rosie Swale' I came across the awful sentence: 'It's a brilliant feeling when my writing goes right – the greatest adrenalin booster in the world and better than any orgasm.'

Now I've never read any of Ms Swale's writing, so I can't really tell or know what it's like when it goes right, but I've always been suspicious and envious of people who actually enjoy the loathsome task. But more to the point I'm extremely worried as to the quality of her orgasms. It all sounds rather like a situation in which Jane Austen might have been writing in a ménage with Adolf Hitler. She also says: 'In the past I've relished my notoriety and sexy image, but now I've reclaimed my body and only do what I want with it.

Nobody's using me again.' Oh, lucky Ms Swale. The last thing I wanted to do was reclaim my body from the last person who laid hands on it and I do so hope someone uses me again. What I wonder about is Ms Swale's unnatural happiness which suffuses her Life in the Day. Just as village idiots wear permanent grins, I feel sure that constantly happy people are not concerned, never reflect and care very little. But good luck to her. I shall continue to be propelled by angst. Nor, unlike Ms Swale, is my idea of heaven to eat, curl up in front of the fire in the arms of the man I love, listen to music and play with the dogs. I might perhaps curl up in the arms of a dog, if I had one, and play with the man I love, if Lester Piggott would permit it, but I'd never be able to concentrate on the music.

What's always puzzled me is how the *Sunday Times* finds such innocuous people to feature. Is there a section headed 'Benign' in the Yellow Pages? All these people wake up in the morning and have a cup of tea or coffee, apparently, and then think about the next chapter of their book. No one, it seems, wakes up to the spine-chilling and persistently commanding ring of the door-bell to find they've run out of both tea and coffee and are therefore unable to entertain the Inland Revenue. They always take their children to school, since they're never divorced, and then they work on their books until lunchtime instead of staring at blank paper until opening time.

One of the questions they asked me at the Middlesex before they trepanned me was, had I ever been jaundiced. I said yes, fifteen years ago. I forgot to tell them it was a chronic condition. But I've opted for this mess instead of sailing round the world, single-handed, collecting owls and doing all the other things people do in the lives-in-the-day-of; and the programme *Opinions*, which goes out on 23 November on Channel 4 in which I've said just why should suitably disgust you if you're up at 11.15 p.m. watching telly and not curled up with your fire, stroking your man and planning your next chapter.

But enough of this nonsense. The Middlesex's generosity with drugs is forcing me yet again to my bed.

The fastest man on four legs

Don't ever be misled by the haggard and depressed face of Lester Piggott. He may be a little shattered at trying to keep his weight down to a unbearably uncomfortable and dehydrated 8st. 6lb., but beneath the saturnine visage there lurks a wit, a brilliant putter-downer of pomposity and, last but not least, the most gifted jockey the world has ever seen.

As a long term aficionado of racing, involved with it professionally and for fun, I view the man with mixed feelings. To me, he's the guvnor sportsman in the world, a man who's dominated his game for even longer than Muhammad Ali, but every time I've met him, I've found little to say.

Suppose you met Messrs Crick and Watson at a cocktail party, it's unlikely that you'd chat to them about DNA. Every time I've ever met Lester the subject of racing has hardly come up, in spite of the fact that I may know slightly more about it than those he might call the men in the street. In fact, the last time I met Lester I told him about a painful scene I witnessed in a betting shop in Soho. An Italian waiter who put a week's wages on a Piggott-ridden horse which got well and truly beaten had an immediate breakdown. He began screaming as soon as the horses passed the post, Lester's being third.

'All my life,' he screamed, 'I've been good to my children and wife. All of them have had the shoes to their feet and the plenty to eat. Now theese bastard Piggott he keel me.' Piggott smiled and said, 'Well, these punters are stupid bastards, aren't they?' Yes, I suppose they are and I suppose he's more than a little amused at the way they follow him blindly.

It's a great pity that Lester stories are mostly unprintable because of the libel laws and they'll remain so until the sad day he weighs in for the last time, but I did like his remark when I spent the day with him last at Newmarket. He rode two horses for Henry Cecil, and at the end of the session he beckoned me back into his Mercedes to take me back to town. As we drove past the end of the gallops where they join the Bury Road in Newmarket I noticed a loose horse. Naïvely I thought the poor brute might break out on to the road and get injured. I turned to Lester and said, 'Look, there's a loose horse. Don't you think we ought to stop and catch it?' Lester turned to me, a wicked smile on his face, and said, 'No. Never catch a loose horse. You can end up all day holding on to the f—— thing.' But I suppose my favourite, and one which sums up Lester's interest in loot was the time he rode a horse in a race sponsored by Kosset Carpets. 'Listen Lester,' they said to him, 'if you win this race we'll give you the usual fee and percentage, but we'll also give you one of those cuddly white cats if you'd like one. Would you like one?' 'No,' he said, 'I'd rather have a monkey.' (Monkey equals £500 in cockney slang.)

When I asked the bluff and usually abrasive Capt Ryan Price his opinion of Piggott, he said, 'Oh my God. What the hell is there to say about the man? He's done everything, he's a bloody genius. The greatest. What else can you say?'

But if you want to hear another expert who can expound at greater length on Piggott, then listen to Farnham 'Maxie' Maxwell, the retired trainer. This tremendously likeable Irishman had a really long association with Piggott. To cut the million words he uttered to me in half an hour down to the gist, it's the activity of the Piggott head that Maxie admires. 'I've known him since he was a tiny boy. The speech impediment and the partial deafness you know. And I'll tell you why I think he's great. He's got a very active brain. When he rode for me he always knew what he had to beat. For example, he'd look at one horse and he'd say to himself that that one will go on and make the running, then he'd look at another and say we'll have to keep in touch with that one. He always knew the opposition so well.'

There was an interesting sidelight to my chat with Maxie. Everyone must know that Piggott's meanness is something of a legend, but not so according to Maxie and his wife Norah. She said, 'He rode a winner for me once and sent back the 10 per cent. and told me to buy a dress with it.' Furthermore, Maxie claims, Lester digs deep into his pockets when there's a subscription for some unlucky person. He also stresses the fact that the grim-faced Lester is a bit of a wit on the quiet.

Mind you, typically and perversely, Piggott wouldn't thank you or me for advertising a soft or sunny streak. I'm positive he enjoys the tales of his penny-pinching and stone-faced outlook. But I'm proud to say I once raised a smile from him. I'd been to Doncaster for the *Sporting Life* and he kindly gave me a lift back to Newmarket. He sat next to his chauffeur studying form and smoking Havanas and, for reasons I have already explained above, I made no attempt to exploit what must have seemed like a heaven-sent opportunity to talk racing. But not a word was uttered during the entire journey. When I got out and thanked him, he eyed me quizzically. 'You're a bit of an idiot, aren't you?' he said (the language was a mite stronger). And, of course, I had to agree. Then, rare and wonderful event, he smiled hugely.

Lester Keith Piggott OBE was born on November 5, 1935, at Wantage. His father Keith then moved to Lambourn and bought him a pony when he was four. 'You couldn't frighten him away from it and he always wanted to raceride. I meant to make him a jockey and it came off,' says Keith. 'It doesn't often, but it certainly came off with him.' Lester became an apprentice to his father and he rode his first winner on The Chase in the Wigan Selling Plate at Haydock Park on August 18, 1948, when he was 12. The next season he won six races and by 1950, although still only 14, he was established, having ridden 52 winners from a total of 404 mounts. At the end of the season he finished 11th in the jockey's table, won that year by Gordon Richards. It soon became apparent that Piggott was determined to win every race he could and he quickly developed a reputation for daredevil and reckless riding. The Stewards took note and he was first reported to them in 1950 after having ridden Barnacle to victory over Royal Oak IV ridden by Scobie Breasley at Newbury. Breasley successfully lodged an objection to Piggott, and Piggott was suspended for the rest of the season although he was allowed to ride in the Cambridgeshire. The next year he rode his first big race winner on the same Barnacle when he won the Great Metropolitan at Epsom.

The steady progression to fame, fortune and glory was now well under way. In 1952 Lester was retained by Mrs J.V. Rank and this was the year that he was to make his first and lasting impression on the Derby, a race which is now 'his' race. He was beaten three-quarters of a length by the Aga Khan's Tulyar. Riding Gay Time, Lester was thrown just past the post and then showed a side of his character which demonstrated the will to win. Completely unembarrassed by the indignity of the situation, Lester wasted no time in lodging an objection against the winner – an almost unheard-of sporting slander as far as the Derby goes – but Mrs Rank wouldn't hear of such a thing.

In 1954 Lester won his first Derby on Never Say Die. But two weeks later, riding Never Say Die again, trouble hit him in a big way, this time in the King Edward VII Stakes at Royal Ascot. Lester rode one of the roughest races many people on the Turf have ever seen. Keith Piggott showed me the film of the race and, from what I could tell, Lester tried for a space on the rails which hardly existed. Gordon Richards on Raleigh, quite rightly, wouldn't give him room to slip through and Lester switched positions to the outside and interfered with the third horse running nearest the stands. Most people who saw the race weren't satisfied that it was all Lester's fault, but the Stewards found it so. In their now historic report they claimed they had 'now taken notice of his dangerous and erratic riding both this season and in previous seasons, and, that in spite of continuous warnings, he had continued to show complete disregard for the Rules of Racing and the safety of other jockeys.' They withdrew his licence to ride and made it a condition that he serve six months with some trainer other than his father. He served that spell in the Turf 'nick' with J.L. Jarvis to whom his first cousin Bill Rickaby was first jockey.

The re-start of his career in 1955 saw the birth of the association between Lester and trainer Noel Murless which lasted for 12 years and must count as one of the most successful flat partnerships in the history of the game. In their first great season, Murless and Piggott won the Derby with Crepello and then completed the Epsom Classic double with the Queen's Carrozza. Two seasons later Piggott won the Oaks with Aly Khan's Petite Etoile and was a colossus who bestrode the best horses in Europe.

In 1960 he became Champion Jockey for the first time when he rode 170 winners from 640 mounts; the feature of the season was his victory on St Paddy in the Derby. In 1961 he rode 164 winners against Scobie Breasley's 171, and the following year he won only 96 winners and was fourth to Breasley. In 1963 he failed by a short head when he rode 175 winners, one fewer than Breasley, but the following year he regained the Championship when he rode 140 winners. Now the genius became palpably apparent. He retained the Championship for the next seven seasons. He rode 160 winners in 1965, 191 winners, his best ever, in 1966, 117 in 1967, 139 in 1968, 163 in 1969 and 162 in both 1970 and 1971. The world could now see, without any argument, his immense power in a finish, using either whip or hands and heels, plus his amazing judgment of pace. He was, indisputably, the guvnor and those who didn't agree were the few that, through bad judgment, judged through their pockets.

In 1966 Lester decided to break his contract with Noel Murless and go freelance. All the pundits told him, or at least voiced opinions to the Press, that this would be the costliest and most disastrous decision of his career. Wrong again. It was with this decision that he was able to undertake to ride Valoris in the 1966 Oaks for Charles Clore. Rumour has it that he rode the filly on the condition that he was given *all* the prize money and not just the 10 per cent. (A filly that wins a Classic today is worth an immediate two or three million pounds at stud.) Whatever the truth of the rumour, Valoris duly obliged.

Now, irrevocably freelance, Lester gave an exhibition lesson in how to keep a horse's stamina up its own sleeve when he won the 1968 Derby on Sir Ivor, who was considered by most people to be unable to stay the one-and-a-half miles distance. Mastery again. In 1970 he won no less than the 'Triple Crown' (2000 Guineas, Derby, St Leger) on Nijinsky and, in the same year, he won yet another Classic, the 1000 Guineas, on Humble Duty, a 'spare' ride he picked up from the Lambourn trainer Peter Walwyn.

Two other Derby stories combine to fill out Lester's profile. One, from 1972, goes some way to explaining why he is, to some, the most exasperating and unpopular jockey in the world, as well as the best. Bill Williamson, the crack Australian jockey was down to ride Vincent O'Brien's horse Roberto, but on the Monday before the race it was announced that Lester would ride the horse. Williamson had, said the reports, been injured. In fact he was fully recovered by the day of the race; nevertheless, Lester kept the ride and went on to win in one of the most exciting Derby finishes in history. Lester was, and remains, ruthless about 'jocking off' another rider if he thinks a mount well worth having.

In 1977 Lester won his eighth Derby on The Minstrel. He had virtually made the race his own. Nevertheless, one might still expect the man to be a little cockahoop. So Captain Ryan Price, the trainer, was somewhat taken aback when, very shortly after dismounting, Lester was seeking him out to discuss plans for the following day when he was to ride an ordinary animal for Price at a second-class meeting. It is testimony to his insatiable will to win.

Last season saw him ride magnificently and this season? Well, there's bound to be the odd miracle or two but, sadly, and I hope to God it's not true, rumour has it that this may well be his last season. He's broken with O'Brien and will be riding freelance as usual, though mainly for the champion trainer Henry Cecil and I've a hunch that he'll be out to prove he's better than ever. Anyway, why stop? Though he is unusually tall for a jockey, he doesn't suffer physically keeping his weight down *quite* as badly as the Press make out – I once saw him tucking in with a vengeance at Annabel's – and, of course he needs the money!

I reckon he must be down to his last £3 million! Speaking personally, my 1981 ambition for 'The long fellow' is for him to ride a winner on a certain two-year-old trained by James Bethell and called Colonel Mad. Meanwhile, I shall rack my brains trying to think of something intelligent to say to him about racing when we next meet, but the likely failure to do so will at least provide a rare sight – old stoneface cracking into a smile.

Trivial pursuit

Six years ago when my last wife sensibly left me I thought never again. Anyway, I'd run out of love and could only splutter from time to time as a car does when it runs out of petrol. So now what really annoys me is that I've been smitten again. The lady in question is a waitress in the Groucho club. How can I describe her? Her hair is very dark brown, almost black, and it looks like silk. Her eyes are like a summer sky and the whites of them are as clear as the sparkle of her teeth behind lips that beg kissing. Between those eyes and that mouth there is the incident of a nose. How God and genes can make perfection out of gristle is nothing short of a miracle. It is the prow of a beautiful ship. And, talking of things maritime, although it is difficult to estimate her body beneath the severe black and white costume obligatory to serve drinks in the Groucho, it would seem to be ample. Not too big, not too skinny. Somewhere half way between the *Sky Lark* and the *Titanic*. To me, she is delicious. But what on earth do you say? So far our conversation has consisted of, 'Good afternoon, sir, what would you like?' and, 'A large vodka, ice and soda, please.' I have explained that my name is Jeff and not sir and I now think that 'sir' is a way of kindly saying 'piss off'.

Th whole business is steeped in paranoia. The more I look at her the more I become aware of my age, weight loss, pending hair loss, pallidness, scruffiness and general physical disintegration. How can I tell her that the inside of the top of my skull is like the ceiling of the Sistine Chapel? Or that my head rings with toccatas and fugues? I can't. All she can see is a twit who spends most of his afternoons dreaming, sometimes snoozing, sometimes arguing in a club. I need a PR badly. Perhaps infatuation like drunkenness is temporary insanity. But I am too old to shoot lines. One is like what one looks like. The *Marie Celeste*.

I know what these people want. Bettina, for that is her name, will end up with a film-maker aged about 30 who drives a Ferrari coupé, one bronzed arm nonchalantly over the driving door, and who lives in a riverside penthouse with a Burmese cat, several gold medallions, a bottle of after-shave, an extremely expensive hi-fi set and no self-doubt whatsoever. All that is so very achievable if you take yourself seriously when you're young – all you have to do is to work hard which any idiot can do – but is it worth it? For Bettina, possibly. Another odd thing is that when I've looked at her in recent days I have noticed that I get slightly short of breath. Of course, I could be having mild coronaries but I don't think so. I think it is because she is so enormously huggable. She has the majesty of an Infanta. Only once have I been temporarily diverted from her presence in the club and that was one evening last week when Germaine Greer called in for refreshment. How some idiot men have got that woman all wrong is beyond belief. The Doctor is quite wonderful and is the only woman I have ever met who doesn't make me resent the fact that she immediately makes me quite aware of the fact that I am an idiot.

Speaking of which I would very much like to know just what they teach at Holland Park Comprehensive School. I went to see my daughter last week and we played a game of Trivial Pursuit. She got a very simple history question which was 'Who succeeded Lenin?' She said, 'Stanley Baldwin.' It's worrying. I used to eat history when I was her age. And now she has her first boyfriend and the fact that he's French is another worry. I suppose he talks like Maurice Chevalier and plants kisses on her all the way up from her hand to her neck. By now she probably thinks we lost Waterloo or that it is merely a railway station. But, more seriously, what shall I do about Bettina? I have nothing to offer except love, a half share in my current account, some vitamin C tablets and a bottle of Veuve Cliquot for breakfast. That is how we start the day, my landlady and I. Perhaps I should apply for a job as a waiter at the Groucho. It would be a sort of marriage. On dear, how very, very much I want to save her from falling into the hands of a really *nice* man. I could give her blood, sweat and tears.